Brief Introduction

This book is aimed at IGCSE and GCSE students of English Literature who are studying Charles Dickens's *Great Expectations*. The focus is on what examiners are looking for, especially since the changes to the curriculum in 2015, and here you will find each chapter covered in detail. We hope this will help you and be a valuable tool in your studies and revision.

Criteria for high marks

Make sure you use appropriate critical language (see glossary of literary terms at the back). You need your argument to be fluent, well-structured and coherent. Stay focused!

Analyse and explore the use of form, structure and the language. Explore how these aspects affect the meaning.

Make connections between texts and look at different interpretations. Explore their strengths and weaknesses. Don't forget to use supporting references to strengthen your argument.

Analyse and explore the context.

Best essay practice

There are so many way to write an essay. Many schools use **PEE** for paragraphs: point/evidence/explain. Others use **PETER**: point/evidence/technique/explain/reader; **PEEL**: point, example, explain, link; **PEEE**: point/evidence/explain/explore. Whichever method you use, make sure you mention the **writer's effects**. This generally is what most students forget to add. You must think of what the writer is trying to achieve by using a particular technique and what is actually achieved. Do not just spot techniques and note them. You may get some credit for using appropriate technology, but unless you can comment on the effect created on the reader and/or the writer's intention, you will miss out on most of the marks available.

Essay planning

In order to write a good essay it is necessary to plan. In fact, it is best to quite formulaic in an exam situation, as you won't have much time to get started. Therefore I will ask you to learn the following acronym: **DATMC (Definition, Application, Terminology, Main, Conclusion**. Some schools call it: **GSLMC (General, Specific, Link, Main, Conclusion)**, but it amounts to the same thing. The first three letters concern the introduction. (Of course, the alternative is to leave some blank lines and write your introduction after you have completed the main body of your essay, but it is probably not advisable for most students).

Let us first look at the following exam question, which is on poetry (of course, the same essay-planning principles apply to essays on novels and plays as well).

9-1 GCSE KEY STUDY NOTES FOR CHARLES DICKENS'S

GREAT EXPECTATIONS –

Revision guide

(All chapters, page-by-page analysis)

by Joe Broadfoot

The right of Joe Broadfoot to be identified as the author of this work has been asserted in accordance with Section 77 of the Copyright, Designs and Patents Act 1988

ISBN-13:
978-1983856488

ISBN-10:
1983856487

CONTENTS

QUESTION: Explore how the poet conveys **feelings** in the poem.

STEP ONE: Identify the **keyword** in the question. (I have already done this, by highlighting it in **bold**). If you are following GSLMC, you now need to make a **general statement** about what feelings are. Alternatively, if you're following DATMC, simply **define** 'feelings'. For example, 'Feelings are emotion states or reactions or vague, irrationals ideas and beliefs'.

STEP TWO: If you are following GSLMC, you now need to make a **specific statement** linking feelings (or whatever else you've defined) to how they appear in the poem. Alternatively, if you're following DATMC, simply define which 'feelings' **apply** in this poem. For example, 'The feelings love, fear and guilt appear in this poem, and are expressed by the speaker in varying degrees.'

STEP THREE: If you are following GSLMC, you now need to make a **link statement** identifying the methods used to convey the feelings (or whatever else you've defined) in the poem. Alternatively, if you're following DATMC, simply define which **techniques** are used to convey 'feelings' in this poem. For example, 'The poet primarily uses alliteration to emphasise his heightened emotional state, while hyperbole and enjambment also help to convey the sense that the speaker is descending into a state of madness.

STEP FOUR: Whether you are following GSLMC or DATMC, the next stage is more or less the same. The main part of the essay involves writing around **six paragraphs**, using whichever variation of PEEE you prefer. In my example, I will use **Point, Evidence, Exploration, Effect** on the listener. To make your essay even stronger, try to use your quotations chronologically. It will be easier for the examiner to follow, which means you are more likely to achieve a higher grade. To be more specific, I recommend that you take and analyse two quotations from the beginning of the poem, two from the middle, and two at the end.

STEP FIVE: Using Carol Ann Duffy's poem, 'Stealing', here's an example of how you could word one of your six paragraphs: **(POINT)** 'Near the beginning of the poem, the speaker's determination is expressed.' **(EVIDENCE)** 'This is achieved through the words: 'Better off dead than giving in'. **(EXPLORATION)**. The use of 'dead' emphasizes how far the speaker is prepared to go in pursuit of what he wants, although there is a sense that he is exaggerating (hyperbole). **(EFFECT)** The listener senses that the speaker may be immature given how prone he is to exaggerate his own bravery.

STEP SIX: After writing five or more paragraphs like the one above, it will be time to write a **conclusion**. In order to do that, it is necessary to sum up your previous points and evaluate them. This is not the time to introduce additional quotations. Here is an example of what I mean: 'To conclude, the poet clearly conveys the speaker's anger. Although the listener will be reluctant to completely sympathise with a thief, there is a sense that the speaker is suffering mentally, which makes him an interesting and partially a sympathetic character. By using a dramatic monologue form, the poet effectively conveys the speaker's mental anguish, which makes it easier to more deeply understand what first appears to be inexplicable acts of violence.

Other tips

Make your studies active!

Don't just sit there reading! Never forget to annotate, annotate and annotate!

All page references refer to the 2000 reprinted paperback edition of *Dr Jekyll and Mr Hyde* published by Wandsworth Classics, London (ISBN: 978-1-85326-061-2).

Great Expectations AQA (New specification starting in 2015)

If you're studying for an AQA qualification in English Literature, there's a good chance your teachers will choose this text to study. There are good reasons for that: it's moralistic in that the text encourages us to think about right and wrong.

Great Expectations is one of the texts listed on Paper 1. More about that particular paper later.

The other paper, Paper 2, needs to be completed in 2 hours 15 minutes. Your writing on the essay will only be part of the exam, however, and for the rest of time you will need to write about poetry: two poems categorised as 'Unseen Poetry' and two poems from the AQA anthology.

AQA have given students a choice of 12 set texts for the Modern Texts section of the exam paper. There are 6 plays: JB Priestley's *An Inspector Calls*, Willy Russell's *Blood Brothers*, Alan Bennett's *The History Boys*, Dennis Kelly's *DNA*, Simon Stephens's script of *The Curious Incident of the Dog* in the *Night-Time*, and Shelagh Delaney's *A Taste of Honey*. Alternatively, students can chose to write on the following 6 novels: William Golding's *Lord of the Flies*, AQA's Anthology called *Telling Tales*, George Orwell's *Animal Farm*, Kazuo

Ishiguro's *Never Let Me Go*, Meera Syal's *Anita and Me*, and Stephen Kelman's *Pigeon English*. Answering one essay question on one of the above is worth a total of 34 marks, which includes 4 for vocabulary, spelling, punctuation and grammar. In other words, this section is worth 21.25% of your total grade at GCSE.

AQA have produced a poetry anthology entitled *Poems, Past and Present*, which includes 30 poems. Rather than study all 30, students are to study one of the two clusters of 15, which concentrate on common themes. There are two themes which students can choose from: Love and relationships, or power and conflict. Within the chosen thematic cluster, students must study all 15 poems and be prepared to write on any of them. Answering this section is worth 18.75% of your total GCSE grade.

The 'unseen poetry' section is more demanding, in that students will not know what to expect. However, as long as they are prepared to comment and compare different poems in terms of their content, theme, structure and language, students should be ready for whatever the exam can throw at them. This section is worth 20% of your total grade at GCSE.

Paper 2 itself makes up 60% of your total grade or, in other words, 96 raw marks. Just under half of those marks, 44 to be exact (27.5% of 60%), can be gained from analysing how the writer uses language, form and structure to create effects. To get a high grade, it is necessary for students to use appropriate literary terms, like metaphors, similes and so on.

AO1 accounts for 36 marks of the total of 96 (22.5% of the 60% for Paper 2, to be exact). To score highly on AO1, students need to provide an informed personal response, using quotations to support their point of view.

AO3 is all about context and, like Paper 1, only 7.5% of the total mark is awarded for this knowledge (12 marks). Similarly, AO4 (which is about spelling, punctuation and grammar) only accounts for 2.5% of the total (4 marks).

Let's return to Paper One now, as it's the main focus of this book. One of the difficulties with Paper 1 is the language. That can't be helped, bearing in mind that part A of the exam paper involves answering questions on Shakespeare, whereas part B is all about the 19th-century novel.

To further complicate things, the education system is in a state of flux: that means we have to be ready for constant change. Of course, everyone had got used to grades A,B and C meaning a pass. It was simple, it was straightforward and nearly everyone understood it. Please be prepared that from this day henceforward, the top grade will now be known as 9. A grade 4 will be a pass, and anything below that will be found and anything above it will be a pass. Hopefully, that's not too confusing for anyone!

Now onto the exam itself. As I said, Paper 1 consists of Shakespeare and the 19th-century novel. Like Paper 2, it is a written closed-book exam (in other words you are not allowed to have the texts with you), which lasts one hour 45 minutes. You can score 64 marks, which amounts to 40% of your GCSE grade.

In section B, students will be expected to write in detail about an extract from the novel they have studied in class and then write about the novel as a whole. Just for the record, the choices of novel are the following: *The Strange Case of Dr Jekyll and Mr Hyde* by Robert Louis Stevenson, *A Christmas Carol* and *Great Expectations* by Charles Dickens, *Jane Eyre* by Charlotte Brontë, *Frankenstein* by Mary Shelley, *Pride and Prejudice* by Jane Austin, and *The Sign of Four* by Sir Arthur Conan Doyle.

Another important thing to consider is the fact that for section B of Paper 1, you will not be assessed on Assessment Objective 4 (AO4), which involves spelling, punctuation, grammar and vocabulary. This will be assessed on section A of Paper 1, which is about Shakespeare, and it will be worth 2.5% of your overall GCSE grade. In terms of raw marks, it is worth 4 out of 64. So for once, we need not concern ourselves with what is affectionately known as 'SPAG' too much on this part of Paper 1.

However, it is necessary to use the correct literary terminology wherever possible to make sure we maximise our marks on Assessment Objective2 (AO2). AO2 tests how well we can analyse language form and structure. Additionally, we are expected to state the effect the writer tried to create and how it impacts on the reader.

This brings me onto Assessment Objective 1 (AO1), which involves you writing a personal response to the text. It is important that you use quotations to backup your points of view. Like AO2, AO1 is worth 15% of your GCSE on Paper 1.

Assessment Objective 3 (AO3) is worth half of that, but nevertheless it is important to comment on context to make sure you get as much of the 7.5% up for grabs as you can.

So just to make myself clear, there are 30 marks available in section B for your answer on the 19th-century novel. Breaking it down even further, you will get 12 marks maximum the backing up your personal opinion with quotations, an additional 12 marks for analysing the writer's choice of words for effect (not forgetting to use appropriate terminology - more on that see the glossary at the back of this book), and six marks for discussing context.

As you can see, we've got a lot to get through so without further ado let's get on with the actual text itself and possible exam questions.

Previous exam questions

Notwithstanding the governmental changes to the grading system, it is still good practice to go over previous exam papers. To make sure that you meet AQA's learning objectives and get a high mark, make sure you go into the exam knowing something about the following:

- the plot

- the characters

- the theme

- selected quotations/details

- exam skills

Please note, all page references refer to the Oxford University Press reissue of 1998 (ISBN 0-19-283359-6).

Chapter 1

In this first-person narrative, we quickly learn that the protagonist's nickname is 'Pip', which would seem to indicate that like a tiny seed, he could grow into a large and fruitful tree. This makes the reader feel quite optimistic that Pip will indeed have 'Great Expectations' (3). Generically, this is a gothic, realist, melodramatic novel of partially autobiographic fiction.

The story begins around between around 1805 to 1809, just a few years before Dickens himself was born. The windswept, desolate setting is reminiscent of the world before creation as described in the Book of Genesis. The gothic churchyard 'overgrown with nettles' reminds us this is a painful place to grow up in.

We feel extra sympathy for Pip because he is an orphan and as the first photographs began to be developed in 1839, he has no idea what his late parents looked like.

During his comic misreading of the gravestones, we are introduced to the idea that this account self-authored by an older Pip, who looks through his younger eyes as a child. This gives the text a dual perspective. Certain themes are already evident: the making or forging of an identity, the search for lost parents, and the misunderstanding of evidence, as Pip draws a 'childish conclusion' that his 'mother was freckled and sickly' (3). Although he is probably mistaken, it does remind the reader that many mothers died during childbirth in the nineteenth century.

On the marshes, Pip soon encounters the threatening Magwith, who is unnamed at this part of the narrative. He is described as 'a fearful man, all in coarse grey, with a great iron on his leg' (4). A lack of verbs in this arresting description helps the reader to see Magwitch as the young Pip sees him.

From the description, we can assume he has escaped from a prison hulk, many of which were moored on rivers, during the nineteenth century.

Through the use of dialogue, Dickens conveys Pip's abject terror in the face of this formidable adversary, who picks the young boy up and tilts him, giving him 'a greater sense of helplessness and danger' (5). The repetition of the word 'tilted' shows that Magwitch is literally turning Pip's world upside down. Metaphorically, this action foreshadows the reversal in Pip's fortune, which happens much later in the novel.

Pip may be terrified, but the reader is not. That is due to dual perspective, which adds distance, making Pip's predicament appear to be somewhat humourous. Although Pip believes it, as readers, we cannot believe that Magwitch's 'young man', who is apparently secreted away, will eat a young boy's 'heart' and 'liver' (6).

The miserable setting serves to add to the feeling of dread produced by the appearance of Magwitch and as Pip retreats from it back to his home, he looks back only to see the 'sky' looking like 'just a row of long angry red lines and dense black lines intermixed' (7). The setting appears to be just as violent as Magwitch, whom Pip has just met.

Pip continues to look back and he can make out 'a gibbet' in the distance (7). He recalls that it 'once held a pirate' (7). Pip's narrative notes that Magwitch is 'limping on towards' the gibbet, which foreshadows the criminal's later fate at the hands of the executioner.

We expect Pip to return to the scene soon, bringing back a 'file' and 'food', as requested by the convict (7).

Chapter Two

Pip's narrative becomes more humorous as he describes how he was brought up 'by hand' by his 'tall and bony' older sister, who is 'twenty years older' than he is (8, 7). We can infer that she is not unaccustomed to striking blows and is generally a heavy-handed person, who Pip assumes forced her husband, Joe Gargery, to 'marry her by hand' (8). Her 'black hair and eyes' and 'redness of skin' are reminiscent of the previous scene, in term of colour (8). In fact, you could associate these colours with the fires of hell.

By contrast to Pip's fiery sister, Joe is described as a placid, 'fair' individual and portrayed in lighter colours 'with curls of flaxen hair' (8). Joe's description makes him appear like an angel, particularly given the juxtaposition of the description of his devilish wife. It sounds as if Joe is 'fair' in terms of meting out justice as well as light-haired.

Although Pip's situation is unenviable, the narrative remains humorous, with a description of the 'Tickler', which belies it gentle name (8). Instead, this violent weapon is wielded by Pip's sister as an instrument of torture to inflict pain on Joe and Pip. This stick is described as 'a wax-ended piece of cane, worn smooth by collision with' Pip's 'tickled frame', which adds more humour to the description of his miserable home life (9). It is almost as if Pip and Joe are determined to enjoy their lives as much as possible, as the word 'tickler' would imply laughter.

Meanwhile, Pip's mission is to bring back some bread for his 'dreadful acquaintance', Magwitch (10). Pip also continues to believe Magwitch's story about an 'ally' lurking out there, who will weake revenge on Pip if he does not deliver food (10). This shows how Pip is naïve and innocent, as even now he has time to reflect on what has happened, he still thinks that Magwitch is accompanied by another escaped criminal, who is even more blood-thirsty. Through the narrative, Dickens portrays Pip as a victim, first to his own naïveté and, secondly, to the dreadful conditions he endures at home. Nevertheless, Pip is brave, as the narrator compares his decision to steal to leaping 'from the top of a high house' or plunging 'into a great depth of water' (11).

Even Joe is mercilessly beaten by his wife, when she takes him 'by the two whiskers' and knocks 'his head for a little while against the wall behind him' (11-12). She is also verbally abusive to Joe, calling him a 'staring great stuck pig' (12). Like Pip, Joe is also being portrayed as a victim. Joe's lack of education is apparent by his use of poor grammar, when he tells Pip: 'you and me is always friends' (12). This implies that Joe is a kind and uncomplicated character.

Dickens continues to use Pip's narrative to decry the return of 'Tar-water' to the medicine cabinets (12). Pip humorously recalls that after this 'restorative' medicine's use, he invariably ends up 'smelling like a new fence' (12). As before, both he and Joe and subject to same abuses, which makes their relationship seem particularly close.

The time setting of 'Christmas Eve' makes the action seem particularly poignant for Pip, who is about to experience a rebirth of sorts (13). His intelligence is apparent through his curiosity to learn, which compels him to ask Mrs Joe 'where the firing comes from' (14). This is also proof of his bravery, as he knows he risks a beating.

Although he has decided that he must steal to feed Magwitch, Pip feels guilty. That guilt is personified when he sneaks downstairs in the dark, as 'every crack in every floorboard' shouts '"Stop thief!" and "Get up Mrs Joe!"' (15).

Nevertheless, Pip steals from the Gargeries, taking the stolen items to 'the misty marshes' (16). The alliterative 'm' draws attention to the gothic nature of the setting.

Chapter 3

The adult reconstruction of the childhood experience continues gothically, as Dickens uses the following simile to describe the damp morning setting: 'as if some goblin had been crying there all night' (16). Already, the writer is foreshadowing the idea that something sad may happen.

Pip's guilt manifests itself again, as now 'cattle came upon' him and he feels he has to answer to 'one black ox, with a white cravat on', who has 'something of a clerical air' about him (16, 17). Clearly, this reference to religion indicates that Pip realises the enormity of his crime: he is breaking one of the Ten Commandments, albeit to honour his promise to Magwitch.

Through the use of Gothic sound imagery, Dickens emphasises how frightened Pip is. The narrator's imagination is running wild, as he describes how Magwitch hears 'some real or fancied sound, some clink upon the river or breathing of beast upon the marsh' (18). The uncertainty adds to the eerie atmosphere.

Magwitch is then compared to a dog as he 'swallowed, or rather snapped up, every mouthful' of the food and drink Pip has given him (19). This animal imagery could indicatesthat the criminal has been treated in a less than humane manner by society.

The dog imagery continues, as Magwitch vows to hunt his fellow escaped prisoner 'down, like a bloodhound' (20). His sense of justice could suggest that he is a morally righteous person, despite his criminal past.

Pip continued fear is emphasised through the straightforward use of repetition of the phrase: 'very much afraid' (21). The narrator is scared to stay with Magwitch, while the latter is working himself up into a 'fierce hurry' as he files 'at his iron like a madman', so Pip finds it expedient to 'slip off' (21).

Chapter 4

The normal joy of a Christmas setting is horribly parodied, as the themes of retribution and punishment are explored in this chapter. Upon his return home, Pip and his 'conscience' are greeted by Mrs Joe's 'salutation': 'And where the deuce ha' you been?' (21). The juxtaposition between the normal expectations of the home comfort of the season and Mrs Joe's harsh outburst remind us how downtrodden Pip is, adding sympathy to his description of his plight. Additionally, the word 'deuce' has associations with the devil, almost as if rather than representing a warm hearth, Mrs Joe is the guardian of the fires of hell.

Mrs Joe, certainly, appears to be less than Godly, as the narrator informs us ironically that she had 'so much to do' that she 'was going to church vicariously; that is to say, Joe and I were going' (22). We can sense Pip's resentment of his sister's hypocrisy, while appreciate the comic effect of his sarcastic joke.

The narrative uses hyperbole to add humour to Pip's plight, as he claims that 'even when I was taken to have a new suit of clothes, the tailor had orders to make them like a kind of Reformatory, and on no account to let me have the free use of my limbs' (23). The reference to a juvenile prison likens Pip to Magwitch, encouraging the reader to make inevitable connections between the two, foreshadowing later events in the novel.

Pip's plight is about to worsen, as 'Mr Wopsle, the clerk at church, was to dine with us', along with Mr Pumblechook (Mr Joe's uncle appropriated by Mrs Joe) and Mr and Mrs Hubble (23). It is revealed that Wopsle 'punished the Amens tremendously', implying that there is no more comfort in church than can be found at home, which continues to add sympathy for Pip's plight.

The narrator describes himself as 'an unfortunate little bull in a Spanish arena', which emphasises how much he suffers (25). Again, the reader cannot help but feel more sympathy for Pip.

We are reminded that the narrative is retrospective, being told by a more mature Pip through the use of sophisticated vocabulary like 'homily', which means sermon and the use of the complex word 'parenthesis' instead of brackets (26). The comic use of metonymy when Mr Wopsle talks of 'swine' while 'pointing his fork' at Pip's 'blushes, as if he were mentioning' his 'christian name' reminds us how abused the narrator is (26). Like the devil, Wopsle is pictured with a 'fork' (26).

Pip's increasing anger towards Wopsle is emphasised by his violent thoughts, as he wants 'to pull' his 'Roman nose' (27). This may be a subtle reference to Dickens's aversion to the Roman Catholic Church.

The anger turns to fear, as Pip thinks he will be discovered and punished for filling 'up the [brandy] bottle from the tar-water jug', now that Pumblechook has drunk from it and fallen into a 'spasmodic whooping-cough dance' (28). This comic moment makes Pip move 'the table, like a Medium of the present day' (28). This is a subtle reference to spiritualism, which had taken hold of Victorian

Britain by the mid-nineteenth century. Dickens dismissed spiritualism as unmitigated quackery.

The tension and the humour of the chapter increase side by side, as Mrs Joe decides to treat Mr Pumblechook to the 'savoury pork pie' that was in the pantry, before Pip stole it to give to Magwitch (29). Dickens uses repetition to add to the significance of the food, which results in Pip running for his 'life' (29). Coincidentally, he runs straight 'into a party of soldiers', which leaves the chapter on a cliff hanger as we can only make an educated guess as to why they have arrived unexpectedly (29).

Chapter 5

Although the arrival 'of a file of soldiers' is very real, it is described in gothic terms as an 'apparition', which adds to the idea that Pip is afraid of the unknown (30). The homonym 'file' reminds us that Pip has stolen Joe's blacksmith tool, which has given Magwitch the opportunity to break free of his shackles (30).

Using a metaphor, the narrator describes how his younger self began to feel less fearful, as 'I collected a little more of my scattered wits' (31). The use of a metaphor emphasises how Pip manages to hold his feelings in check, now the military have put the pie 'in the background' (31).

Pumblechook, meanwhile, is described as getting the credit' for 'handing' out wine to the sergeant 'in a gush of joviality' (32). The narrative makes Pumblechook appear to be foolish and hypocritical, as he is manipulated by the sergeant's compliments into being so generous with the Gargeries' wine.

The men, apart from Pumblechook and Hubble, take their 'leave of the ladies', which shows how the pursuit of criminals would not have been regarded as suitable for women at that time (33).

Meanwhile, Pip whispers 'treasonably' to Joe that he hopes they 'shan't find' the criminals (33). Joe feels the same, so you get the sense that the law is an ass, with a drunken sergeant pursuing Magwitch and another escaped convict.

Through the use of an apt simile, the writer demonstrates how close to Joe Pip is, when his 'heart' is described as 'thumping like a blacksmith' (34).

The convicts are described inhumanly as 'two wild beasts', once apprehended by the sergeant (35).

However, the soldiers are also described animalistically as 'like deer', which is a simile that implies that they are no better and are just as unthinking (35).

The narrator reveals how much he is on the side of Magwitch, by using the personal pronoun 'my' before the word 'convict' (36). This links Pip directly to the criminal and thereby foreshadows what happens later in the novel.

Meanwhile, although both convicts are nameless at this point, adding tension, we will later find out that the 'bruised' one is a 'gentleman' called Compeyson (36). Magwitch has left him 'bruised' but not 'murdered', so it appears that the former is honourable, despite being a criminal (36).

The narrator looks at Magwitch 'eagerly' to assure him of his 'innocence' (37). At the time, the young Pip 'did not understand' the look he received in return from Magwitch, but from an adult perspective, the older Pip relates that it was 'attentive' (37). Once again, Dickens is foreshadowing the idea that the two characters will have a lot to do with each other in the future.

The young Pip's terror is shown by how he 'had hold of Joe's hand now', as the convicts are marched back to the Hulks (38). Pip is probably still afraid that the revelation that he stole the file and the pie will come to light. He need not have worried, as Magwitch claims responsibility for taking 'some broken wittles [...] a dram of liquor, and a pie' (39). Magwitch uses the word 'took' rather than stole to describe how he acquired these articles, which allows him to remain honest, despite removing the blame from Pip (40).

Joe's christian charity elicits a click in Magwitch's 'throat', which indicates that he is feeling emotional (39). This depiction of this particular criminal is largely sympathetic.

Meanwhile, Magwitch has to return to the Hulk, which is 'like a wicked Noah's ark' (40). By using a Biblical simile and inverting it, Dickens effectively reminds us all, particularly perhaps church-goers, not to judge others.

Chapter 6

Pip's decision to keep a guilty secret has marked the beginning of his loss of innocence. Inevitably, it will lead him away from Joe, although ironically, it is the 'fear of losing Joe's confidence' that motivates Pip to avoid 'frank disclosure' (40).

Through the use of repetition of the word 'cowardly', the writer demonstrates how Pip straightforwardly recognises his own shortcomings. This makes him a sympathetic character to the reader.

Pip is unceremoniously put to bed by his sister, after the night's excitement, 'with such a strong hand that I seemed to have fifty boots on'. Through the use of hyperbole, the writer conveys Pip's sense of injustice, while making the account humorous for the enjoyment of the reader.

Chapter 7

The narrator tells us how ignorant he was as a youngster and blames some of it on how he 'bound' by the 'Catechism' of christian teaching (42). Dickens rebelled against the formality of much church teaching, and this seems to a be a not-so-subtle criticism of the question and answer format of the oral catechism, which was often used to educate the young.

Another topical point is raised by the text, when the narrator mentions how any money raised by his hard work at menial tasks would be deposited in 'a money-box', which would be 'contributed towards the liquidation of the National Debt' (43). The use of hyperbole emphasises how, from Pip's point of view, the money vanishes into a black hole, as enormous as the huge debt racked up by Britain during the war with Napoleon that concluded in 1815.

Later, we hear of Biddy, for the first time, who, like Pip, is an 'orphan' and 'had been brought up hand', without her mother's milk (43). She appears to be Pip's female double, which ties in with doppelgängers, which were prevalent in the gothic genre. She is Wopsle's 'great-aunt's granddaughter'. She appears to be nothing like Wopsle, so the hereditary side of human nature seems to be disregarded by Dickens (43). Instead, the writer seems to believe that environmental issues make Pip, who does not share a common bloodline, similar to Biddy. For example, they both have hands that 'always wanted washing' (43).

However, Biddy is more educated than Pip, helping him to struggle 'through the alphabet as if it had been a bramble bush' (44). This shows how important education is to Pip and how he is prepared to go through the pain barrier to improve himself.

This determination makes him unlike Joe, whose 'education, like steam, was yet in its infancy' (45). By comparing Joe's education to how slow steam trains used to run during the early part of the nineteenth century makes it sound as if he doesn't have the technical capacity to learn faster.

We hear that Joe's father 'didn't make objections' to his son's neglect of his education in favour of work (46). Of course, child labour was common at the time.

Pip, meanwhile, fears Joe has deluded himself into believing that Mrs Joe 'is a fine figure of a woman' (47). Joe relates the tale of how Pip was welcomed at 'the forge' too, when the marriage with Mrs Joe took place (47). The word 'forge' could also imply that the bond between Pip and Joe is as strong as two different types of metal being melted together.

Both of them share a similar plight, as they live in fear of Mrs Joe. The narrator admits he had some 'shadowy idea' or 'hope' that 'Joe had divorced' her (49). The word 'shadowy' gives the thought an element of the gothic about it.

The narrator admits he developed 'a new admiration of Joe that night', after their frank talk (49). This is juxtaposed with the resentment he feels towards his sister, who repeats that she hopes Pip 'won't be Pompeyed' or pampered (50). Perhaps the word 'Pompeyed' is a subtle reference to the Roman general Pompey, who achieved a lot in his life but was ultimately betrayed. In a sense, that could foreshadow Pip's end, to some degree.

Mrs Joe later pounces upon Pip 'like an eagle on a lamb', which may indicate that it is simply her nature that drives her to maliciously attack her brother (51). Using a list, Dickens reveals the trials and tribulations that Pip is subject to: 'I was soaped, and kneaded, and towelled, and thumped, and harrowed, and rasped' (52). The accumulation of the near brutality is emphasised by the repetition of the word 'and'. Pip appears to be an innocent, passive victim of domestic violence, although the narrative uses hyperbole to achieve some comedy from the tragic situation.

Chapter 8

Some of the setting described at Mr Pumblechook's corn-chandler and seedsman business premises is speculative, as the narrator wonders when he peeps into drawers 'whether the flower-seeds and bulbs ever wanted of a fine day to break out of those jails, and bloom' (32). Likewise, Pip is in a prison of sorts, where he is subject to punishment and is prevented from blooming due to a lack of education.

Around Pumblechook's, very little is going on in terms of business. Significantly, only 'the watchmaker' seems actively and usefully employed (53). The writer draws our attention to the importance of time. Later, we will discover how Miss Havisham (who Pip is about to meet) cannot move on in her life, as for her time has stopped.

The theme of incarceration repeats itself, as Pumblechook and Pip arrive at Miss Havisham's Satis House. The narrator notes the 'great many iron bars' and even the courtyard, which would normally be associated with freedom and even courting, is 'barred' (54). Through repetition, the writer successfully conveys the idea that Miss Havisham has shut herself away almost completely.

The prison imagery of the Hulks is re-evoked, as the narrator refers to 'the cold wind' that 'seemed to blow colder there [...] and it made a shrill noise [...] like the noise of wind in the rigging of a ship at sea

(55). The use of pathetic fallacy to convey the narrator's sense of foreboding is mixed with the gothic to create add to the idea that Pip is afraid about what might happen.

The narrator meets Estella for the first time and she takes him to Miss Havisham's room and tells him to 'go in' (56). The dual narrative perspective is evident as Pip apologises for his limited appreciation of the 'forms and uses' of the furniture (56). This draws attention to the fact that, like Miss Havisham, the furniture is losing a recognisable form and is useless to the 'strangest lady' he has ever seen (56).

Time stands still here, as we are told 'her watch had stopped at twenty to nine', which is a time replicated by the clock (57). There is no life in the 'ghastly wax-work' that Pip sees before him (57). The writer's horrific description adds to the tension, as we wonder what will happen to Pip.

Just as cold if not colder than Miss Havisham is Estella, who is described through the candle she bears as 'a light' that that 'came along the dark passage like a star' (58). To Pip, she is like a heavenly being (which is also indicated by her name, as the word 'stellar' concerns stars): beautiful, but cold and distant.

Estella cruelly makes Pip aware and ashamed of his 'coarse hands' and 'thick boots' when they play the card game: 'beggar my neighbour' (59). The game represents the selfish acquisition of wealth, which as a charitable philanthropist, Dickens was opposed to.

Pip's honesty is preyed upon by Miss Havisham, who asks him to tell her what he thinks of Estella. The writer uses anaphora to make Pip's simplistic for comments more impactful, as he repeats: 'I think she is...' three times (60). We learn that she is 'proud', 'pretty' and 'insulting' (60). Dickens uses a tricolon to make sure that the reader has a memorable picture of Estella's attributes and lack of. This technique was particularly useful in serialisations, as readers would have to wait between the publication of episodes, so would need the characters to be as memorable as possible.

The emotions Pip feels are asyndetically listed, as the narrator reveals he felt: 'humiliated, hurt, spurned, offended, angry, sorry' (61). He eats as if he 'were a dog in disgrace', which links him to Magwitch from an earlier scene. Like Magwitch, Pip is being judged harshly.

Pip rids himself of his anger somewhat by 'kicking them into the brewery wall, and twisting them out of' his 'hair' (62). This shows that he is a survivor, despite the perceived 'injustice' (62).

Meanwhile, his obsession with Estella is clear as 'she seemed to be everywhere' (63). Foreshadowing the future, he sees 'a figure hanging' (63). This place is associated with death and 'terror', which the writer repeats three times to add tension (63).

The chapter ends with Pip bemoaning his 'coarse' hands, 'thick' boots and his 'despicable habit of calling knaves Jacks' (64). The latter point had already been flagged up by Estella, but it seems to simply show how he is buying into her snobbery, when perhaps he should be questioning her values as, no matter what you call them, Jacks and knaves amount to the same thing. Estella has been a poor guide to Pip but, nevertheless, she is a motivating force to him, as he wishes he could impress her.

Chapter 9

The word 'coarse' has resonated with Pip, as he feels 'there would be something coarse and treacherous' in telling Mrs Joe how Miss Havisham really is (64). He feels a strange sense of loyalty towards Miss Havisham, perhaps because he aspires to be more like her and Estella.

Pip now has a double life, as he has been invited back to play with Estella again. When asked how well he got on by Pumblechook, he is evasive, answering: 'Pretty well, sir' (65). Pip seems to feel a sense of power for the first time in his life.

This sense of power grows, as Pip begins to compose more expansive lies, telling Pumblechook that Miss Havisham is 'very tall and dark' and has 'four dogs', which 'fought for veal cutlets out of a silver basket' (66). Once again, there is the motif of the dog, which is associated with Magwitch and Pip, but this time the animal seems to make good, as he is eating with three others from a 'silver' basket.

Pip appears to relish this chance to exercise his imagination further, as he goes on to say that they 'played with flags' and 'swords' (67). He tells Pumblechook and Mrs Joe that Estella's flag was 'blue', his was 'red', and Miss Havisham's was 'sprinkled all over with little gold stars' (67). Symbolically, these colours could indicate that Estella is distant like the blue sky, the reddened Pip is embarrassed and angry, and Miss Havisham is obsessed with Estella (hence the stars).

When Joe appears, Pip confides in him, telling him, colloquially: 'it ain't true' (68). Joe is mortified, describing the lies as 'awful' (69). Nevertheless, Joe tries to build up Pip's confidence by telling him how 'oncommon' he is, by virtue of his 'small' stature and ability as a 'scholar' (69). Joe further encourages Pip, by telling him he needs to begin 'at A' before working 'his way to Z', like even the 'king upon his throne' had to do 'when he were an unpromoted prince' (70). Through this analogy, Pip feels 'encouraged' (70).

The narrator reveals that this day was the making of him and uses direct address to warn the reader: 'Pause you who read this, and think for a moment of the long chain of iron or gold, of thorns or flowers, that would never have bound you, but for the formation of the first link' (71). Like in 'A Christmas Carol', life's events are turned into links in a chain, which bind people to their fate. In 'Great Expectations', this metaphor works particularly well, as it also relates to Joe's job as a blacksmith. It appears that Pip wants to move from a life with the Gargeries of 'iron' and 'thorns' to a life of 'gold' and 'flowers', which could represent money and romance.

Chapter 10

Pip's determination to improve his education begins with his visit to 'Mr Wopsle's great-aunt's at night' to 'get out of Biddy everything she knew' (71). Although Pip may sound a little selfish, in that he will only reveal that he has 'a particular reason for wishing to get on in life', Biddy is so 'obliging' (71). Pip quickly realizes it will 'take time, to become uncommon' given how riotous the school is, but his determination is evident as he still resolves to 'try it' (72). The negative word 'uncommon' indicates that he is turning from his natural state of being common and will not necessarily achieve an improvement if he makes it to his goal.

The word 'common' is repeated, as Pip is under instructions from his sister to pick Joe up from the Jolly Bargemen, where he finds him in 'the common room' (73). With him, buying him 'rum', a drink often associated with piracy and skullduggery, he sees a man wearing a 'flapping broad-brimmed traveller's hat' and a 'cunning expression' (74).

The strange takes an interest in Pip, thinking he is Joe's 'nevvy' or nephew (75). Joe reveals that they are not blood related and Mr Wopsle, also present, tries to clarify the relationship by quoting from the 'Table of Kindred and Affinity' before regaling them with a 'snarling passage' Shakespeare's 'Richard the Third' (75). We may presume the speech in question begins with: 'I must be married to my brother's daughter', which is outlawed by the aforementioned Table' (4.2.60). This proves how hypocritical Wopsle is.

The narrator reveals that the strange man is indeed Magwitch, as he stirs his rum with 'Joe's file' (76). Before, Joe and Pip leave, Magwitch offers Pip 'a bright new shilling' (76). This foreshadows the generosity that Pip will be the beneficiary of later, as well as implying that the future is 'bright'.

It turns out that Magwitch has wrapped the shilling in 'two fat sweltering one-pound notes', which Joe unsuccessfully tries to return to the former owner. Gold and silver were in short supply between 1797 and 1821, and 1825-26, so these notes were legal tender for that time. Clearly, we can guess that date of the setting as a result, which is corroborated by an authorised dramatised version of the text, which starts when Pip is 15 years-old with the year being something between 1815 and 1820.

Chapter 11

The 'rank ruin of cabbage-stalks' with 'a new growth [...] out of shape' in the 'neglected garden' at Satis House seems to represent Miss Havisham's mind and body, although the new growth could represent Estella (78).

Once Pip enters a room containing 'three ladies [...] and one gentleman, he notices the conversation has 'stopped' (79). He describes all these guests as 'toadies and humbugs', the latter being a word that Scrooge uses frequently in 'A Christmas Carol' to mean fake, while the former are servile parasites (79). Presumably, these people (Camilla, Cousin Raymond and Sarah Pocket) are hoping to inherit Miss Havisham's fortune.

After hearing 'a distant bell', Estella takes Pip out and asks him if she is 'insulting' (80). When Pip replies: 'Not so much as you were last time', she slaps him (80). In this way, Dickens presents her as a cold psychopath, incapable of human warmth.

A new character is introduced to us, who we later find out is the lawyer, Jaggers. He is 'a burly man of an exceedingly dark complexion, with an exceedingly large head and a correspondingly large hand' (81). He is presented to use as an almost grotesque figure, who would not be out of place in hell, with his 'bushy black eyebrows', which seem to have lives of their own (81). These hairy personified features draw attention to his eyes, which are 'deep' set and 'disagreeably sharp and suspicious' (81).

After escaping Jagger's' clutches, another depressing scene presents itself, as Pip is instructed to go into a room which 'had an airless smell that was oppressive' (82). It represents how lifeless Miss Havisham has become and is intended to become her crypt. In it, Pip sees Miss Havisham's 'bride cake', which is a symbol of her morbid and poisoned mind (83). It is also a visible expression of her embittered self-destructive psyche.

One of the aforementioned toadies, Miss Pocket, compliments Miss Havisham, telling her 'how well' she looks (84). The latter can see straight through the false flattery and she replies: 'I am yellow skin and bone' (84). Juxtaposed against such liars, Miss Havisham appears to be exceedingly honest, so may begin to become a sympathetic character to readers.

Miss Pocket is presented, meanwhile, as 'a little dry brown corrugated old woman, with a small face that might have been made of walnut-shells, and a large mouth like a cat's without the whiskers' (85). The imagery conveys the idea that she has a hard exterior like a nut and is rather predatory like a cat.

However, Miss Havisham has the measure of her covetous relatives and dismisses them. Before leaving, Camilla complains: 'it's very hard to be told one wants to feast on one's relations - as if one was a Giant - and to be told go' (86). The 'Giant' could be a reference to Cronos, from Greek mythology, who ate his own children and maimed his own father.

After they leave, Miss Havisham tells Pip it is her birthday and how she won't 'suffer it to be spoken of' (87). The gothic atmosphere is enhanced by the personification of 'the heavy darkness that brooded in' the room's 'remoter corners' (87).

After he has played with Estella, Pip is permitted 'to wander about' and he takes himself to the garden (88). Here, he exchanges 'a broad stare with a pale young gentleman with red eyelids and light hair', who invites him to 'fight' (88, 89). After Pip makes short work of his adversary, he only feels 'a gloomy satisfaction' in his 'victory' (90). He compliments his opponent, who seems 'so brave and innocent' (90). Pip regards himself thereafter as 'a species of savage young wolf, or other wild beast' (90). This animal imagery reminds the reader that Pip does not have delusions of grandeur, despite his great expectations.

Pip is almost rewarded for his efforts, as Estella offers him 'her cheek' to kiss (91). However, Pip realises that it is 'worth nothing' (91). This is juxtaposed with the scene that meets his eyes as he returns home and see 'Joe's furnace [...] flinging a path of fire across the road' (91). This fire imagery could imply that Joe offers human warmth, which is not present at Miss Havisham's. It could also mean that Joe, in a sense, stands in the way of Pip's road to his great expectations.

Chapter 12

Pip's belief in karma is evident, as he feels he will receive 'punishment' for how he has beaten up the 'pale young gentleman' (91). He twists his 'imagination into a thousand tangles' over Herbert Pocket, whose name is not revealed at this stage of the narrative (92). The personification of Pip's imagination shows how worried he is that there will be repercussions from his fight.

The narrative condenses time, as Pip reveals he is 'going to sum up a period of at least eight to ten months', as he reveals that Miss Havisham did nothing to improve his education and seemed to 'prefer' him 'being ignorant' (93). This gives the reader a clue that Miss Havisham would be a very unlikely benefactor.

Pip is, meanwhile, dismissive of Pumblechook, whom he calls an 'ass', and how he would meet with Mrs Joe to discuss Pip in 'such nonsensical speculations about Miss Havisham' (94, 95). This foreshadows what happens later in the novel, as the slightly hypocritical Pip also speculates about the person or persons who help to improve his prospects.

However, it seems as if Miss Havisham might be finally showing a genuine interest in Pip, when she asks him to bring along Joe and his 'indentures', which is paperwork regarding Pip's pending apprenticeship (96). The writer leaves us with that speculative cliffhanger and tying it with the idea the ever-patient Joe may be indulging in some 'speculation' of his own, regarding his troubled marriage.

Chapter 13

Joe has decided his 'court-suit' is necessary for the trip to Miss Havisham's (97). This shows how in awe he is of those of a higher class and reminds us how little class mobility existed at the time. The suit also links to the theme of crime, justice and punishment and indicates that Joe is respectful of the law.

Joe's respect for those whom he regards as social superiors is evident in that 'throughout the interview' he persists 'in addressing' Pip rather than Miss Havisham (98).

Nevertheless, Pip associates his indenture as an apprentice blacksmith as a form of death, as the narrator remarks that Joe decides to 'adapt his epitaph to the occasion' (99). Joe continues to address Pip, even when Miss Havisham hands over twenty five guineas for the 'premium' he has earned for his 'master' (99).

When Joe and Pip finally leave Miss Havisham's house, the former continues to utter the word: 'astonishing' (100). It is as if Joe's limited vocabulary cannot cope with the sights he has seen at Miss Haversham, which is a feature adding to the almost unspeakable gothic nature of the narrative.

Like Pip, Joe begins by lying to Mrs Joe about what came to pass at Miss Havisham. He tells his wife: 'Miss Havisham [...] made it wery partick'ler that we should give her - were it compliments or respects, Pip?' (101). The fact that he consults Pip implies that the experience has traumatised him so much he can't remember the truth.

However, he does roughly remember the sum of money, 'five-and-twenty pound', handed over to him by Miss Havisham, as his honest nature prevails (102).

As recommended by Pumblechook, all four go directly to the Town Hall to have Pip 'bound apprentice to Joe' without further ado (102). While there, Pip is erroneously thought to be a criminal by some of the crowd gathered there, and one hands him 'a tract ornamented with a woodcut of a malevolent young man fitted up with a perfect sausage-shop of fetters, and entitled TO BE READ IN

MY CELL' (103). The writer appears to be having a sly dig at the Tractarian Movement, which began in the 1830s and threatened to move Protestantism closer to the Roman Catholic Church, a move that Dickens was very much against.

Pip admits, at the end of the chapter, that he feels 'truly wretched' as he is no longer a blacksmith in his heart (104).

Chapter 14

This is a retrospective chapter, which reflects on how feelings change. The narrator comments how 'it is a most miserable thing to feel ashamed of home' (104). Pip has been transformed by his time with Miss Havisham and Estella and now wants more than what he would have settled with at the start of the narrative. His perception has altered in 'a single year' in that 'now, it was all coarse and common' (105). The alliteration adds to the impression that Pip is cursing his station.

Pip admits he is 'haunted by the fear that she [Estella] would, sooner or later, find me out, with a black face' (106). Being a blacksmith is not something he can be proud of, after spending so much time with richer people with higher social status than the Gargeries.

Chapter 15

The setting for Pip's education 'at Mr Wopsle's great-aunt's room' is left vague and the description of it is as underdeveloped as his knowledge, at this stage in the narrative, despite Biddy's best efforts (106). Her attempt to teach him a 'comic song', which begins: 'When first I went to Lunnon town sirs' foreshadows Pip's journey to London, which occurs later in the plot (106).

Pip's educational fate seems inextricably linked to Magwitch, as the setting chose for his Sunday studies is 'the old Battery out on the marshes', which is where he first encounters the escaped convict (107). Nevertheless, he finds himself thinking of 'Miss Havisham and Estella', as the desire to be more like them is the motivational force for his studies (107).

Pip takes these day dreams and the idea of a visit to Satis House to Joe, who advises him to 'make a end on it' (107). Joe adds: 'Me to the North, and you to the South' to indicate that he believes that fate is leading Pip away from Miss Havisham and Estella (107). Ironically, we will discover that Pip's great expectations will take him away from Joe instead.

Joe believes that Pip should take 'a present' to Satis House, but the narrator clearly thinks it would not be well received (109). Pip asks for 'a half-holiday' so he can make the trip, and Joe assents (109).

We meet another character as the narrative progresses called 'Dolge' Orlick, which some critics believe is onomatopoeic of someone who traipses through mud (110). Orlick is described as 'a journeyman', which suggests he is travelling employee, who can choose his boss as he is no longer apprenticed to anyone (110). He is described as 'a broad-shouldered loose-limbed swarthy fellow of great strength, never in a hurry, and always slouching' (110). This vivid description gives us the impression of an indolent man, who could be dangerous as 'he always beat his sparks' at the forge in Pip's direction (110). There is certainly a lot of burning resentment in Orlick towards Pip, despite the lack of open 'hostility' (110). This makes it appear as if Orlick is a brooding, formidable adversary, waiting his time to strike. He is likened to the biblical figure of Cain, who killed his own brother in a pique of jealousy.

This jealousy is soon presented by Dickens, Orlick (speaking of himself as if he is 'an ancient person') says to Joe that: 'If Young Pip has a half-holiday, do as much for Old Orlick' (111). Joe allows both to have a half day off, much to Mrs Joe's chagrin.

In the argument that follows between Orlick and Mrs Joe, the pair trade insults, Orlick calling her a 'foul shrew', or a nag (112). This puts Joe in an invidious position, as he is no longer able to keep the peace. He locks horns with Orlick, whom he knocks down 'among the coal dust' (113). Once again, Orlick is associated with filth, but he recovers his composure despite 'a slit in one' of his 'nostrils' and the 'two giants' share 'a pot of beer' which appears 'from the Jolly Boatman' pub (113).

This fight does not augur well for Pip's prospects at Miss Havisham's and he is disappointed to discover that Estella is being educated 'abroad' (114). After a quick meeting, Miss Havisham dismisses him allowing him to visit in future on his 'birthday', which reminds us of the importance of dates and times to her (114).

Meanwhile, Pip uses the rest of his half day to wander 'along the High-street' thinking about what he would buy if he 'were a gentleman' (114). Whilst doing this, he sees Mr Wopsle reading 'the affecting tragedy of George Barnwell', which is an eighteenth century prose version of a ballad about a man who robs his employer and kills his uncle because of a woman he has been seduced by (114). The reader can sense how Pip may have a guilty conscience about how he only cares about Estella and may be prepared to ride roughshod over Joe's feelings to get her. Pip virtually admits his guilt by revealing that what 'stung' him was 'the identification of the whole affair' of Barnwell with himself (115). Meanwhile, it could be argued that the Barnwell story foreshadows much of what is about to happen.

The setting becomes 'very dark' as Mr Wopsle and Pip set off for home (115). On the way, they meet the 'slouching' Orlick, who admits he 'must have been pretty close behind' them (115). It is almost as if he hoped to catch Pip or somebody else alone and the scene is made more threatening by the 'boom' of the 'signal cannon' (115).

As the walk past 'the Three Jolly Bargemen', they discovered a 'commotion' (116, 117). The upshot is Mrs Joe has been attacked while Joe was out. The chapter ends on a mysterious 'whodunnit'-style cliffhanger, as Mrs Joe lies 'without sense or movement' having been knocked down by 'some unknown hand' (117).

Chapter 16

The enquiry as to what happened begins to unravel as the narrator informs us that Joe was at 'the Three Jolly Bargemen, smoking his pipe, from a quarter after eight o'clock to a quarter before ten' (117). The narrative continues in the same vein as we discover that 'when Joe went home at five minutes before ten, he found her [Mrs Joe]' (117). The assailant's weapon was 'a convict's leg iron', which makes the readers think it must be an escaped criminal who committed the act of violence. However, as it was 'filed asunder some time ago', it cannot be 'either of the two convicts who had escaped last night' (118). Although he had no real input into the attack, Pip feels guilt, as he admits: 'It was horrible to think that I had provided the weapon, however undesignedly' (118). This makes him appear more sympathetically to the reader.

With his sister laying 'very ill in bed', Biddy becomes a 'suitable attendant' for her (120). Biddy moves in and is a 'blessing to Joe', who can now disappear to the pub 'now and then for a change' (121). Biddy also interprets the now mute Mrs Joe's rudimentary drawing to mean she was attacked by Orlick.

However, once Orlick is summoned from the work place, Mrs Joe simply is possessed by 'the greatest anxiety to be on good terms with him'. Therefore, the reader is still left with a cliffhanger, wondering why Mrs Joe continually draws 'the hammer on her slate' to summon Orlick to her bedside.

Chapter 17

Each time that Pip visits Miss Havisham, he receives 'a guinea' (122). The narrator describes the setting at Satis House as 'unchanging', which matches his 'regular routine of apprenticeship-life' (122). However, he is still 'bewildered' and therefore fascinated by 'the full old house', which influences him enough to make him 'hate' his trade and 'be ashamed of home' (122).

Still unable to see Estella, he is ready to condemn the 'common' Biddy, although he admits 'her hair grew bright and neat' and 'she was pleasant and wholesome and sweet-tempered' (123). The repetition of the connective 'and' makes the list of her attributes appear as if Pip cannot help himself adding just one more compliment, despite his feelings for Estella, to whom Biddy is shabby in comparison. He is even impressed with Biddy's 'pretty eyes' as the writer begins to present her as an alternative love interest for his protagonist (123).

Biddy is presented as the archetypal, ideal Victorian woman: 'quietly sewing' (124). Consequently, Pip (like contemporary readers) is attracted and invites Biddy for a 'quiet walk on the marshes next Sunday' (124). The setting seems more appropriate for villainy than romance, as Pip encountered Magwitch there earlier in the narrative. Nevertheless, it is 'summer-time', so the gothic setting is not as threatening as it is in winter (125).

We find out from their chat that Pip is full of self-pity, as he bemoans how 'coarse and common' he is before telling Biddy how he wants to 'be a gentleman on her [Estella's] account' (126). Meanwhile, we are not given access to Biddy's thoughts, although we can infer that she is trying to be a good friend to Pip, realising that he is too in love with Estella to be obtainable as a possible lover. This may be why when Pip asks if he is 'good enough' for her, she replies comically with a hint of irony that she is 'not over-particular' (126). She seems to realise that his ambition to be 'gentleman' will inevitably take him away from her (127). Biddy adds a little mysteriously and modestly: 'If your first teacher (dear! such a poor one, and so much in need of being taught herself!) had been your teacher at the present time, she thinks she knows what lesson she would set' (127). We are left guessing what it would be, but it appears to be that Estella is 'not worth gaining over' (126). Biddy realises 'it's of no use now', as Pip has his heart set on becoming a gentleman in order to win Estella over.

As they continue their walk in this 'beautiful' setting, Pip wonders whether he isn't 'more naturally and wholesomely situated, after all, in these circumstances, than playing beggar my neighbour by candlelight in the room with stopped clocks, and being despised by Estella' (128). Pip has effectively put Estella on a pedestal, as an ideal love match and as someone to vaguely aspire to be with. Estella is not as real a person as Biddy, but maybe Pip has penchant for the unnatural, as he admits frankly and immodestly to Biddy: 'If I could only get myself to fall in love with you' (128).

On the way home, the pair meet Orlick, who emerges from the 'ooze' (129). He wants to 'see' them home, but Biddy asks Pip to decline the invitation as she's afraid 'he likes' her (129). Pip considers it an 'outrage' to himself, although he pretends 'it makes no difference' to him (129). These contradictory feelings show how mixed up Pip is as an individual, as he aspire to win over the distant and cold Estella by becoming a gentleman, while risking losing Biddy as a romantic interest. The problem is his aspiration for Estella makes Biddy appear as less desirable in comparison.

It could be argued that Pip is ad capricious as Estella, in that he admits he had 'states and seasons when' he was 'clear that Biddy was immeasurably better than Estella, and that the plain honest working life to which' he 'was born, had nothing in it to be ashamed of' (130). The question is should he give up a blacksmith's life which he knows can give him 'sufficient means of self-respect and happiness' or aim to become a gentleman, which seems unobtainable without some form of divine intervention (130)?

Chapter 18

Time is condensed as we now reach the 'fourth year' of Pip's 'apprenticeship to Joe' on a 'Saturday night' at the Three Jolly Bargemen (130).

Mr Wopsle's theatrical performance of a court scene in the pub foreshadows the lawyer Jaggers's reappearance. Dickens uses grotesque, exaggerated and vivid characterisation to make his characters memorable, which is essential for serialised novels. Readers may be able to remember Jaggers from his distinctive mannerism of biting 'the side of a great forefinger' although initially he is presented as 'a strange gentleman' (131).

Jaggers proceeds to interrogate Wopsle, making the latter look quite ignorant, ridiculous and even a devil worshipper as he says: 'You may read the Lord's Prayer backwards' (132). Jaggers with 'his air of authority' exposes Wopsle as 'not the man we had thought him' (133). The lawyer has already impressed upon the others that he is force to be reckoned with.

Although the reader may have already recognised Jaggers, Pip has only just 'recognised him as the gentleman I had met on the stairs' at Satis House (134). The 'stairs' are symbolic of Pip's attempt to ascend to the status of a gentleman. Finally, the title of the novel is mentioned as Jaggers asks Joe to 'cancel' Pip's 'indentures', as the young man 'has great expectations' (135).

Jaggers begins to mention the 'profound secret' about Pip's benefactor and how it is 'positively prohibited' for him to make inquiries as to the identity of the said person (136). Another 'condition' of his 'great expectations' is to 'always bear the name of Pip' (136). Pip becomes aware of 'a singing' in his 'ears', so excited is he at the prospect of realising his wildest dreams (136).

Pip is told of 'a certain tutor', called Matthew Pocket, who may be able able to help him to become a gentleman (137). Jaggers then hands over 'twenty guineas' so that Pip can buy 'some new clothes' before meeting Matthew Pocket's son in London (138). The pace of the narrative is increasing, as Pip's great expectations suddenly become realistic.

Jaggers then offers Joe 'compensation' for 'the loss of the little child' Pip (139). However, Joe's relationship with Pip transcends 'Money'. As readers, we are aware of the retrospective nature of the narrative being told by an older, wiser Pip when we read the line: 'O dear good faithful tender Joe, I feel the loving tremble of your hand upon my arm, as solemnly this day as if it had been the rustle of an angel's wing!' (139). Once again, Joe is portrayed as angelic. However, Joe is ready to clash with Jaggers, Pip's far-from-angelic new guardian, who continues to insist on offering 'a present' of compensation, until the narrator 'drew Joe away' (139).

Joe's grief at losing Pip is apparent when they return home, as he assumes the foetal position: 'holding his knees tight' by the fire (140). The seating arrangement at home is significant as 'Joe sat next Biddy', which foreshadows how relationships will change with the realisation of Pip's great expectations (140).

Rather than becoming as 'cheerful' as Biddy and Joe become as the news of the fantastic opportunity to become a gentleman sinks in, Pip becomes 'quite gloomy' (141).

Aptly, Pip is portrayed looking up at 'the very stars' as he counts down the days until his move to London. The 'stars' represent his good fortune and the distant and cold Estella.

Already, Pip seems to have delusions of grandeur, as he insists that he does not want 'to be stared at by all the people' in his 'new clothes', despite Joe suggesting it would be a 'compliment' to the Hubbles, Wopsle and those at the Jolly Bargemen (142).

We get the impression that the old Pip has died, as when he looks to the 'open window' (representing his new-found freedom), he sees 'light wreaths from Joe's pipe floating there' (143). The word 'wreaths' is funereal imagery and it is significant that Joe's pipe is providing them, as he is most affected by the loss of the young Pip. Joe is losing a long-term close companion as well as his apprentice.

Chapter 19

The Sunday 'morning' setting seems significant as Pip thinks about embarking on his journey in hope of realising his dream of becoming a gentleman, as it indicates the birth of a new week and a new day (143). A new horizon beckons and a new day will dawn in Pip's history. Pip's 'indentures' are burnt, which makes him feel 'free' before his departure in six days' time (144).

Pip also mulls over the past. Given what happens later, it is ironic that he feels ashamed of his 'companionship with the fugitive' Magwitch, as their fates are inextricably linked (144).

Meanwhile, it appears that Pip's path will lead him further from Joe, whom he wishes was 'better qualified for a rise in station' (145). Pip cannot seem to accept Joe for what he is.

Biddy explains to Pip that Joe 'may be too proud to let anyone take him out of a place that he is competent to fill, and fills well, and with respect' (146). Pip thinks that Biddy is 'envious' of his 'rise in fortune', so seems more than reluctant to believe that she is right (146). Pip repeatedly tells her 'it's a bad side of human nature', and uses 'a virtuous and superior tone' when addressing her (147). He even extends his 'clemency to Biddy', which shows how he has become snobbish, since finding out about his 'bright fortunes' (147).

Pip's news about coming 'into a handsome property' to 'Mr Trabb, the tailor' results in a completely different treatment to what Pip is accustomed to (148). Trabb's boy is less respectful, but nevertheless Pip feels 'the stupendous power of money' lays even this 'vagabond' on his back, 'morally' (149).

Pumblechook is similarly affected and wants to 'shake hands' and drink with Pip (150). Despite all the problems Pip has had with Mrs Joe, he proposes a toast. Pip is forgiving towards his sister, as he suggests: 'We'll drink to her health' (151). Pumblechook now falls 'to reposing such great confidence in' Pip, now that the latter's fortunes have significantly improved (152). In fact, 'the sunny street', which is part of the setting, represents Pip's improved prospects (153).

Before embarking on the journey, Pip decides to visit Miss Havisham, who has been transformed into a 'fairy godmother' in his imagination (154). However, the grim, gothic setting complete with 'cobwebs' prevents the reader from being taken in (155).

On the eve of his departure, Pip admits he, Joe and Biddy, 'were all very low [...] in spirits (156). When he leaves the house, he sees Biddy and Joe 'throwing an old shoe' after him to wish him luck (157).

Chapter 20

Part two is about Pip's arrival in London, which in some ways resembles Chatham's marshy landscape of dirt, gibbets, complete with other symbols of crime and punishment. Pip's first impressions upon alighting are that Cheapside is 'rather ugly, crooked, narrow, and dirty' (161).

Once Pip arrives at Jaggers's office in Little Britain, he is left in a gothic room to await the lawyer, who is 'in Court' (162). The narrator describes it as 'a most dismal place; the skylight, eccentrically patched like a broken head, and the distorted adjoining houses looking as if they had twisted themselves to peep down at me through it' (162). Through personification, the writer makes the environment appear to be actively hostile.

Rather than simply wait, Pip tells the clerk that he will 'take a turn in the air', which results in him wandering into the nearby Smithfield, which a market area known for its butchers. The narrator describes it as a 'shameful place, being all asmear with filth and fat and blood and foam' (163). This description makes London seem like a violent place and echoes Pumblechook's prediction of the butchery of Pip the pig, whom he likens to a 'four-footed squeaker' (27).

Pip continues his grim tour of London and is invited into Newgate Prison by 'an exceedingly dirty and partially drink minister of justice' to 'hear a trial' (164). In a sense, Pip is also on trial metaphorically, as he has much to contend with. Pip declines the invitation, but is still shown 'the gallows', which are reminiscent of the gibbet on the marshes and the vision of Miss Havisham hanging at Satis House (164).

When he returns to Jaggers's, Pip discovers that he is not the only one awaiting the lawyer's return. One Jewish man seems to be praising Jaggers in a rhyme, by saying that all other lawyers are 'Cag-Maggerth', which means 'rotten meat' (165). The use of meat imagery, especially so soon after the description of Smithfield, reminds the reader what a brutal place London is.

When Jaggers does appear, he fends off the Jewish people waiting for him with various threats, such as: 'Wemmick shall give you your money back' (166). Characteristically, when he becomes 'irate', Jaggers throws 'his forefinger' at a 'terrified client' (167). The writer has to give his characters grotesque idiosyncrasies to make them memorable to readers, which is vitally important for commercial serialisation.

When Jaggers finally finds time for Pip, he uses law imagery to warn the young man that although his 'credit' is 'good', he must guard against 'outrunning the constable' or overspending (168). Jaggers states that he will 'check' Pip's 'bills', presumably to ensure that any overspending is stopped before it has catastrophic consequences (168). Jaggers is pessimistic about the chances of avoiding overspending, saying to Pip: 'Of course you'll go wrong' (168).

Jaggers stops Pip from getting 'a coach', instead allowing his clerk, Wemmick, to 'walk round with him' to '"Barnard's Inn," to young Mr Pocket's rooms, where a bed had been sent in' (169, 168). Already, Jaggers is controlling Pip's destiny and is trying to prevent the young man from spending money unnecessarily.

Chapter 21

The narrator describes Jaggers's clerk, Wemmick, as 'a dry man, rather short in stature, with a square wooden face, whose expression seems to have been imperfectly chipped out with a dull-edged chisel' (169). This description implies that Wemmick has had to adapt to hard knocks of life in London, which could be likened to wood being shaped with a chisel that is not necessarily fit for purpose. The impact of these metaphorical blows seem to have taken their toll on Wemmick face, which may be quite resilient, judging by its 'square' shape.

As they approach Barnard's Inn, in Hammersmith (which can be linked with Joe's blacksmith profession), Pip misinterprets the place in a similar way to how he misread the tombstones in chapter one. The narrator erroneously assumes that Barnard's Inn is 'an hotel kept by Mr Barnard' (170).

He seems disappointed to discover 'Barnard to be a disembodied spirit, or a fiction, and his inn the dingiest collection of shabby buildings ever squeezed together in a rank corner as a club for Tom-cats' (171). This gothic imagery effectively portrays London as a depressing place to be.

Being from the countryside, or the county of Kent to be more precise, Pip is 'in the habit of shaking hands' (172). This motif recurs in chapter nineteen, when Pumblechook says: 'May I, may I...' (143). This custom takes Wemmick by surprise as he admits: 'I have got so out of it!' This admission implies that London is so hectic and impersonal that people no longer have time to shake hands. It reminds the reader how unaccustomed Pip is to the ways of London and how vulnerable he is as an innocent newcomer to a busy, unfeeling city.

Even the building is unwelcoming, as Pip is nearly 'beheaded' by 'the staircase window' which comes 'down like a guillotine' (172). The writer makes the scenery come alive to make the environment seem particularly threatening to Pip.

At least, while 'Mr Pocket, Junior's, idea of Shortly' is not Pip's (given he has to wait for the former to 'Return shortly' as per a note left for him), the young man's agreeable smile' presumably makes the narrator feel more welcome (172, 171, 173).

Using the dialogue, and Mr Pocket, Junior more specifically, the writer describes the scene: 'This is our sitting room - just such chairs and tables and carpet and so forth' (173). It sounds like temporary accommodation, which has been cobbled together at the last minute.

The chapter ends with a revelation as Pip identifies his new friend as 'the pale young gentleman' whom he fought with a Satis House (173). This is an effective cliff hanger for a serialisation, as the readers will wonder if the pair will fight again or will be able to let bygones be bygones.

Chapter 22

We discover that 'the pale young gentleman's name' is Mr Herbert Pocket and Pip and he shake 'hands warmly' (174). The hand shake motif appears again, perhaps, because a firm one can indicate that you are dealing with a trusted gentleman.

Herbert tells Pip that he considers Estella to be 'a Tartar' and not necessarily unlike Miss Havisham in that respect (174). This means Estella is formidably savage and ill-tempered, not unlike the Mongolian and Turkic descendants of Genghis Khan, who ruled over much of western Asia and eastern Europe until the eighteenth century. This link to Genghis Khan tells the reader that Estella is merciless.

Herbert is very important to the plot, as he fills narrative gaps. For example, Herbert tells Pip that Estella is 'adopted' rather than a blood relation of Miss Havisham (175). This must make Pip and the reader realise together that he has something in common with her, in that she was not raised by her parents.

Herbert insists on being called by his christian name, while Pip tells him in 'exchange' that his name is 'Philip' (176). This goes against what he promised to his unknown benefactor: that he should always be known as Pip. Herbert asks if he can call him 'Handel' instead, as there is a 'charming piece of music by Handel, called the Harmonious Blacksmith' (176, 177). Like Pip, the eighteenth-century composer, Handel, was born elsewhere but ended up settling in London.

The pair proceed to eat what 'seemed to' Pip then, in this retrospective narrative, to be 'a very Lord Mayor's Feast' (177). This reminds the reader that like Dick Whittington, who journeyed to London to eventually become its mayor, Pip has also arrived in the hope that he can further himself. This links to the 'finger-post' motif at the end of Pip's village in Kent, which is also suggestive of Dick Whittington and the idea that dreams can come true in London (157). It could be argued that the finger-post is accusing Pip, in a similar way to how Jaggers uses his finger to point at people, and it could act as an ironic commentary on and a reversal of the normal 'rags to riches' story. It should be noted that the finger-post does not seem to be pointing to London, so it may symbolise whether or not it is in Pip's best interests to make the trip.

Now that he is in London, Herbert has effectively taken him under his wing, informing him and the reader about how Miss Havisham became 'an heiress' and how a so-called gentleman was her downfall (178). On the latter topic, Herbert asserts (like his father) that 'no varnish can hide the grain of wood', but nevertheless, Miss Havisham 'passionately loved' this man (179). The wood imagery reminds us of Wemmick, so we may wonder if he is gentleman or not.

Continuing his tale and hence performing an important narrative function for the reader, Herbert tells Pip that the man 'wrote her a letter' instead of turning up for their wedding (180).

Unfortunately for Pip, Herbert cannot shed much more light on Estella, which adds to the veil of mystery already surrounding her for the reader. However, Herbert can tell Pip that his job: 'A capitalist - an Insurer of Ships' (181). This links Herbert to the writer's son, Charley Dickens, who was employed in a similar line of business.

Our first indication that Pip questions what Herbert says comes when the latter explains that he has not 'begin insuring yet', adding that he is 'looking about' him (182). Pip thinks that Herbert's employment therefore does not have 'a profitable appearance', but good manner (of a gentleman-to-be) make him 'defer to his [Herbert's] experience' (182). To put this into context, Dickens is using Herbert to criticise his son, Charley, whom he felt was a little foolish when it came to business.

Using the narrator's 'moderate computation', the narrative condenses time to let us know that 'many months' have passed since Pip 'left Joe and Biddy' (183). The word 'computation' indicates a mathematical calculation, so links well with the previous topic of Herbert's employment at the 'counting-house' (182). The narrative returns to the Herbert's place of work, as Pip accompanies him and describes it as 'a grimy presence in all particulars' (184). It is more gothic than glamorous.

After this visit, the pair visit Hammersmith and Mr Pocket Senior's house, where they meet Herbert's mother, who receives Pip 'with an appearance of amiable dignity'. To put this in context, Dickens may have based this character on his wife, who had separated from relatively recently in 1858. Like Mrs Pocket, Mrs Dickens was often considered amiable and the narrative treats this fictional character comically, while presenting her as deserving of respect and pity.

Some of the comedy of this chaotic household is presented through the narrator's observation that 'Mr and Mrs Pocket's children were not growing up or being brought up, but were tumbling up' (184). Meanwhile, Mrs Pocket's identifying feature for contemporary readers of the serialisation is her propensity to drop her 'pocket-handkerchief'. Indeed, the nurse, Flopson, remarks after picking it up: 'if that don't make seven times!' (185).

Given this backdrop, the narrator is unsurprised to discover that Mr Pocket is 'a gentleman with a rather perplexed expression of face, and with his very grey hair disordered on his head', he seems unable to 'quite see his way to putting anything straight' (186). This description makes the end of the chapter a cliff-hanger of sorts, as it's hard to imagine how this disorganised man can whip Pip into shape and turn him into a gentleman.

Chapter 23

Mr Pocket reveals that he is not an 'alarming personage' and addresses his wife as 'Belinda', so through realistic dialogue we discover her first name (186).

Belinda Pocket's obsession with marrying 'a title', apparently is the result of being 'the only daughter of a certain quite accidental deceased Knight, who had invented for himself a conviction that his deceased father would have been made a Baronet but for somebody's determined opposition' (187). By writing such a complex sentence (of which the example above is only a portion), Dickens conveys the idea that Mrs Pocket's delusions of grandeur are ridiculous. Perhaps, the writer is alluding contextually to his father-in-law, George Hogarth, who worked for a famous knight: Sir Walter

Scott. Meanwhile, this obsession of hers is a caricature of Pip's quest to be a gentleman.

Herbert then takes Pip to his room, which is not described much. However, Pip is introduced to the other 'occupants, by name Drummle and Startop' (188). Drummle is described as 'an old-looking young man of a heavy order of architecture' and he is portrayed as 'whistling' (188). Immediately, the reader gets the impression that Drummle is physically strong, yet carefree and irresponsible. The name 'Startop' meanwhile reminds the reader of Estella and foreshadows a possible love match between her and Drummle.

We discover that Drummle's 'christian name' is 'Bentley'. This makes it appear as if there is nothing straightforward about this man, as he sounds bent or corrupt. The 'drum' part of the name 'Drummle', meanwhile, hints at the violence of playing the instrument above.

We also discover that he is 'actually the next heir but one to a baronetcy', which seems to indicate that Mrs Pocket (with her view on titles) should be suitably impressed (189). In reply to Mrs Pocket's inquiries, 'Drummle didn't say much, but in his limited way [...] he spoke as one of the elect, and recognised Mrs Pocket as a woman and a sister'

(190). Ironically, this line echoes the contemporary anti-slavery slogan: 'Am I not a man and a brother?' Of course, Drummle has been born metaphorically with a silver spoon in his mouth, so knows nothing of servitude.

The 'toady neighbour', Mrs Coiler, meanwhile, is apparently based on Dickens's mother-in-law (190). The snake imagery of the name makes it obvious that the writer disapproved of his wife's mother, particularly after his marital problems.

In contrast to the negative portrayals of Drummle and Mrs Coiler, Mr Pocket is characterised by his tendency to 'lift himself up by the hair', which makes him easily identifiable for readers in serialisation format (191). This action is repeated again and again to make sure that readers can remember. For example, Mr Pocket gets 'his hands in his hair again, and this time really' does 'lift himself some inches out of his chair' (192). Later, Pocket 'with one very strong effort to lift himself up by the hair' dismisses the 'hopeless' topic he was asking his child-minders about (193).

Mr Pocket's theatrical presentation continues, as he drops into the stance of 'the Dying Gladiator', which is a statue in Rome of a figure propping himself up on one arm (194), Byron described this gladiator as: 'Butcher'd to make a Roman holiday', so we can feel a certain amount of sympathy likewise for the plight of Mr Pocket.

Chapter 24

We get the impression that Pip is unsettled, when the narrator tells us that he 'had gone backwards and forwards to London several times' in the first 'two or three days, when' he had 'established' himself in his room (194).

After 'a long talk' with Herbert, it occurs to Pip that his 'life would be agreeably varied' if he can 'retain' his 'bedroom in Barnard's Inn' (194, 195). This indicates that Pip is easily bored.

In order to make this happen, he needs to ask his guardian, Jaggers, for some money. Jaggers questions Pip in a style reminiscent of Pumblechook's arithmetical inquisition in chapter eight. For example, Jaggers asks Pip: 'Four times five; will that do?' (196). It is difficult to tell whether Jaggers is mocking Pip or is trying to educate him. Judging by Jaggers's creaking boots that seem to laugh 'in a dry and suspicious way', we cannot discount the former idea.

Pip admits to Wemmick that he hardly knows 'what to make of Jaggers's manner', to which the clerk replies: 'it's not personal; it's professional: only professional' (196). The repetition emphasises how important work is in London and how impersonal everything is there.

Wemmick describes Jaggers as 'deep [...] as Australia', which is an interesting simile given that, at the time, the country was used as a prison colony for Britain (197). AIt also foreshadows what happens later in the narrative.

Wemmick shows Pip the 'two odious casts with the twitchy leer upon them', which had already caught his eye (198). We can infer that Jaggers is quite happy to mingle with criminals, given that he has kept these death masks as personal momentos.

Although Wemmick admits that curios, such as these, are not worth much, he tells Pip that it is always wise to 'get hold of portable property' (199). This seems to be his mantra or 'guiding-star' for survival in the city (199).

Wemmick then invites Pip to his home in Walworth, before advising him to 'look at his [Jaggers's] housekeeper' when he gets the chance (199). Pip is assured that he will be invited to Jaggers's also and, that if he looks at the housekeeper, he will see 'a wild beast tamed' (199).

Before the chapter ends, Wemmick takes Pip to see Jaggers 'at it' in court (200). He cannot fail to be impressed by Jaggers's manner and his 'single bite of his finger', which seems to wield so much power (200). We get the impression that Jaggers is a powerful man, who is not to be trifled with.

Chapter 25

Bentley Drummle is described as 'so sulky a fellow that he even took up a book as if its writer had done him an injury' (200). We get the impression that he is ignorant and has no aspirations to improve himself. This completely sets him at odds with Pip, making him appear like a natural adversary or antagonist.

In fact, Drummle is portrayed as a sneaky character in a way that is reminiscent of another potential Pip adversary, Orlick, who is often spotted creeping behind the narrator in a murky setting. Likewise, Drummle 'would always creep in-shore like some uncomfortable amphibious creature' after a spot of 'boating' (201). The simile makes Drummle appear to be less than human.

The narrator admits he 'contracted expensive habits', but he remains different to Drummle the 'dolt', in that he still wants to improve himself, as he can still 'feel' his 'deficiencies' (202). Although he goes 'through good and evil', Pip sticks 'to his books', which seem to ground him (202).

Pip then goes to Wemmick's home in Walworth on foot, and is given more reason to respect his guardian as the clerk tells him that Jaggers 'gives it out publicly, "I want to see the man who will rob me"' (203). This shows how arrogant Jaggers is, while making him seem a formidable force, worthy of respect.

Wemmick's home turns out to be 'gothic' and a 'little wooden cottage' (204). The house is isolated by the 'bridge', which can be hoisted up to 'cut off communication' with the outside world (204). It makes the reader think of the phrase that the Englishman's home is his castle, with this mock drawbridge over a tiny, ineffective moat (which only measures 'four feet' in width and 'two' in depth) (204). However, symbolically, it cuts off the domestic Wemmick from his profession.

Wemmick's fantasy of owning 'the Castle' in the middle of London is highlighted when he asks Pip to suppose 'the little place besieged' and imagine how long it would hold out because of the 'provisions' on site (205). The cottage gives Wemmick an escape from the hard reality of life in the London legal profession.

The domestic side of Wemmick is so different to his clerical side, and even his father, 'Aged', indulges in this castle fantasy (206). When Wemmick lets the 'gunfire' off at nine o'clock for their 'great nightly ceremony', he claims 'it's the Aged's treat' (206). The sound imagery may remind the reader of how the Hulks fire cannon when prisoners have escaped.

Pip stays the night in a tiny room, which seems reminiscent of what he's been used to in Chatham: a 'little turret bedroom' (207). This makes Wemmick's cottage seem extremely homely, despite its idiosyncrasies.

The next morning when they return to 'Little Britain', Wemmick's 'mouth tightened into a post-office again' (207). This reminds the reader there is a clear differentiation between public professional and personal life in London. Once at work, Wemmick 'looked as unconscious of his Walworth property as if the Castle and the drawbridge and the arbour and the lake and the fountain and the Aged, had all been blown into space together by the last discharge of the Stinger (208). The repetition of 'and' reminds the reader of how much of Wemmick's personal life he has to put to one side and forget, once he is in the workplace.

Chapter 26

Jaggers's habit of 'washing his hands with scented soap' is likely to be a subtle biblical reference to Pontius Pilate, who washed his hands, not wanting to take responsibility for the crucifixion of Jesus Christ (208). The habit certainly implies that Jaggers has a guilty conscience or that he finds his job disgusting and filthy, and wants to wash the dirt off. In fact, his home is also grimy and gloomy, as Pip discovers on his visit there with Herbert, Startop and Drummle, is 'dolefully in want of painting, and with dirty windows' (209).

Strangely, Jaggers professes an instant 'like' of Drummle, describing him as 'the spider' and 'the blotchy, sprawly, sulky fellow' (210). Perhaps it suggests that Drummle is a potential criminal, as

Jaggers spends a lot of time associating with the underworld.

The narrator, meanwhile, as per Wemmick's instructions, observes Jaggers's housekeeper, who is described as: 'rather tall, of a lithe nimble figure, extremely pale, with large faded eyes, and a quantity of streaming hair' (210). She is reminiscent of the typical Victorian mad woman locked in the attic, that features in novels, such as 'Jane Eyre'. The narrator likens her to 'the faces' he 'had seen rise out of the Witches' cauldron' in Shakespeare's 'Macbeth' (210). This description makes her appear to be like Miss Havisham, Estella's foster mother, who is also described as a witch.

The narrator adds that 'whenever she was in the room, she kept her eyes attentively on my guardian' (211). It appears that she is beholden to him in some way.

Jaggers exhibits her like some oddity in a Victorian freak show, by insisting that she shows the assembled guests her 'wrist' (212). This she does, under protest. We discover her name is Molly and that Jaggers has 'never' seen 'stronger' hands than hers (212). It seems a strange fixation on his part.

The narrative focus shifts to Drummle, and we discover that he is a user. He has borrowed money from Startrop and then is 'amused at his being so weak to lend it' (213). This negative portrayal of Drummle in the ensuing argument with Pip, that takes a violent turn when he tries to throw a 'large glass' at Startop, makes the reader loathe this character (214). Hence, it adds tension to the plot.

Mystery is added by Jaggers's advice that Pip should 'keep as clear of' Drummle as he can (215). However, Jaggers maintains that he likes 'that Spider though' (214). It is almost as if Jaggers is literally the devil's advocate.

Chapter 27

This chapter is known for its mix of pathos and humour. It begins with Biddy's letter to Pip, asking if he can make himself available to meet Joe, who will be visiting London with Wopsle. She signs off as 'your ever obliged and affectionate "Servant," Biddy. This makes her seem like Pip's social inferior and therefore makes any prospect of marriage impossible (215).

Pip feels relieved that his brother-in-law is visiting him at Barnard's Inn and not at Hammersmith, as 'consequently [Joe] would not fall in Bentley Drummle's way' (216). Clearly, Pip is worried that Joe will be associated with him and mocked by Drummle.

The narrator's admission, that 'our worse weaknesses and meannesses are usually committed for the sake of the people whom we most despise', seems to explain why Pip employs 'a boy in boots' (216). Through this 'avenging phantom', the writer parodies Pip's self-importance and desire of social distinction (216). However, Pip has to pay for his delusions of grandeur.

Upon his arrival, Joe also pays in embarrassment, as he tries desperately to meet what he presumes are Pip's great expectations of guests. Joe proceeds to shake both of Pip's hands 'straight up and down, as if' he 'had been the last patented Pump' (217). The motif of shaking hands allows the writer to portray Joe as an earnest and honest friend to Pip.

The writer injects humour into the scene, while conveying Joe's insecurity, by describing his hat as 'like a bird's nest with eggs in it' (217). This simile conveys the idea that the hat is suddenly precious to Joe, who wants to cling onto something familiar in this strange environment. It is like a comfort blanket to him and the scene is reminiscent of when he meets Miss Havisham, earlier in the narrative.

Joe tells Pip that Wopsle has given up the church to pursue a career 'playacting' (217). It appears that Joe has seen Wopsle performing a role in Shakespeare's 'Hamlet', as he says: 'if the ghost of a man's own father cannot be allowed to claim his attention, what can, Sir?' (218). Joe speaks with more foresight than he realises as Pip should be more grounded and have less airs and graces, when Joe visits, if he wants to make his old friend feel less uncomfortable.

Meanwhile, Joe's hat continues to symbolise his social insecurity and he has to juggle with it as much as he does his syntax. He tries to place it on 'the mantelpiece' and before that 'on an extreme corner of the chimney-piece, from which it ever afterwards fell off at intervals' (219). The relatively high places where he tries to hang his hat seem to symbolise the social heights that Pip has reached, while the hat's inability to grip anything shows how ill at ease Joe is.

Personification continues to be used by the writer to achieve a comic effect, as Joe has to show 'the greatest skill', which is 'very like that exacted by wicket-keeping' to keep his hat in check (220). The reference to cricket, which was and is generally regarded as an upper or middle class sport, reminds the reader how out of his depth Joe is.

Although retrospectively, Pip realises that he was to blame for Joe's awkwardness, at the time, Pip 'had neither the good sense nor the good feeling to know that' (220). At least, the older Pip seems to have learned from his mistakes, making him a sympathetic character.

Before he leaves, Joe imparts some vital information about Estella, as she 'has come home and would be glad to see' Pip, according to Miss Havisham (221).

Interestingly, Joe refers to the narrator as 'Sir [...] and Pip', which reminds us of the dual narrative and how much London has changed the apprentice, he once knew so well (222).

Joe almost apologetically tells Pip how awkward he feels when he says: 'I'm wrong out of the forge, the kitchen, or off th' meshes' (222). Although Joe means the marshes, this spelling is significant, as it puns on the idea that Pip is 'enmeshed' in his past

Chapter 28

In this retrospective narrative, Pip is critical of his invented 'reasons' and 'excuses' for 'putting up at the Blue Boar' instead of 'at Joe's', although his guilty 'repentance' makes him decide that he must 'repair' to his 'town next day' (223). Pip is compounding his guilt with financial foolishness and false pride, as he seems to be out to prove to everyone that he is indeed a gentleman and is still not ready to meet Joe in a way that will not cause embarrassment to his brother-in-law.

Before he leaves for Chatham, Herbert warns Pip that 'Convicts' will be taken down to 'the dockyards' on the same 'stage-coach' (224). Pip says while he doesn't 'mind' convicts, he 'can't pretend' that he likes them either (224). It seems to be Pip's destiny to be close to criminals and, in particular, Magwitch, who is on the same trip. Pip knows 'his half-closed eye at one glance' (224). This makes Magwitch appear to look like a stereotypical villain, which ties in with Victorian ideas of physiognomy.

Pip describes the convicts on the stage-coach as having a 'coarse mangy ungainly outer surface, as if they were lower animals'. It appears that Pip's snobbery has no bounds.

As they leave, Herbert calls out: 'Good-by, Handel!' which contravenes the terms of the agreement with the unknown benefactor, who insisted that Pip should be known as 'Pip' and not by any other name (226). However, Magwitch hasn't recognised Pip so, in that sense, the name Handel puts him in potentially less danger.

The dog imagery continues to be used to describe Magwitch and the other convict, as 'they gradually growled themselves out', after complaining about the 'mudbank, mist, swamp and work' that they will reencounter at 'the wicked Noah's Ark' (227). Before disembarking, they are told to 'Give way', which the narrator says is 'like an order to dogs' (227). This implies that the convicts behave like animals because they are treated like that.

Upon his arrival at the Blue Boar, Pip is dismayed to read in 'a dirty old copy of a local newspaper' that 'a highly-respected individual not entirely unconnected with the corn and seed trade' was his 'Mentor' (228). Although Pumblechook and Pip are not named, their identities are clear. Pip seems most uncomfortable with the idea that this kind of rumour is rife. Of course, Dickens himself had not unfounded rumours to contend with, following his separation from his wife.

Chapter 29

Pip's romantic assumptions are evident in this chapter, as he wildly speculates that as Miss Havisham 'had adopted Estella, she had as good as adopted' him (229). He believes he can break the spell which Satis House is labouring under and uses chivalrous language to show this, when he says that Miss Havisham 'reserved it due me to restore the desolate house' and 'in short, do all the shining deeds of the young Knight of romance, and marry the Princess' (229).

However, when Pip arrives at Satis House, he is shocked to discover that Orlick is 'porter at Miss Havisham's door' (230). Orlick represents another symbolic barrier for Pip to overcome, and could be likened to hell's gatekeeper. The narrator uses animal imagery to describe Orlick's quarters, which 'look like a cage for a human dormouse' (231). This simile conveys the idea that Orlick is lazy.

Once admitted into Miss Havisham's presence, Pip kisses her hand 'as if' she 'were a queen' (232). He seems to have great respect for the upper classes.

Pip appears to be more confident now and he observes an 'elegant lady', whom he finds out is a grownup Estella. Pip complains that Estella still treats him 'like a boy', but still allows her to lure and influence him (233). For example, Estella's remark about 'unfit company' makes him lose 'any lingering intention left, of going to see Joe' (234).

Estella claims she has 'no heart', yet she looks 'attentively' at Pip, which implies attraction (235). Pip needs little encouragement, even romanticising 'the ruined garden' with its 'most precious flowers' (236).

When the couple return from their walk in the garden, Miss Havisham repeatedly implores Pip to 'love her [Estella]' (237).

Jaggers appears and once the lawyer starts interrogating Pip, Miss Havisham says: 'Jaggers [...] leave my Pip alone' (238). The possessive pronoun shows how she is beginning to think she has created Pip, as well as Estella. jagger even cross-examines 'his very wine' (239). This behaviour makes Pip 'nervous' (240).

Pip wonders if she 'awaken' Estella's heart, which makes him an incurable romantic.

Chapter 30

Pip's fear that Orlick not 'being the right sort of man to fill a post of trust at Miss Havisham's' is not initially taken seriously by Jaggers, but eventually the lawyer says he will 'pay our friend off' (241). Quite whose money he will use is not altogether clear, although that does not seem to be the reason why Pip advocates 'a little delay' (241). Jaggers, however, is too forceful for Pip and Orlick presumably, as he says: I should like to see him argue the question with me' (241).

While Jaggers is dealing with Orlick, Pip decides he wants 'a walk' and, on it, 'Fate' throws him 'in the way of that unlimited miscreant Trabb's boy', who proceeds to prostrate 'himself in the dust', having spotted the narrator (242). Much to Pip's embarrassment, Trabb's boy continues with his madcap antics, which draws 'a knot of spectators' (243). The word 'knot' could imply that Pip feels like he has a lump in his stomach, so much is he disturbed by Trabb's boy. Pip seems to realise that Trabb's boy is mocking him, especially when he repeatedly says: 'Don't know yah!' This phrase shows how snobbish Pip appears to the people of the town. Perhaps Pip deserves this parody of his social pretensions, especially as he has chosen not to visit his one true friend, Joe.

Rather than doing the right thing, Pip decides to send 'a penitential codfish' and a 'barrel of oysters to Joe (as reparation for not having gone [...]) (244). At this stage in this Bildungsroman, Pip clearly had not learned how to treat people.

Instead, he remains obsessed with Estella, so much so that he informs an unsurprised Herbert that he 'doubly' adores her (245). He wonders how he can impress her as a jobless gentleman, and Herbert replies that he should call himself 'a good fellow' (245). Nevertheless, Pip believes that 'Fortune alone has raised' him (245). Again, he is unwilling to credit Joe with his upbringing. The personification of 'Fortune' makes it obvious that Pip believes in luck and is neglecting to see the contribution made by people like Biddy and Joe, who both really care about him.

Pip continues to be self-indulgent, revealing his insecurity to Herbert about how his financial well-being depends 'on the constancy of one person (naming no person)' (246). Herbert sensibly tells him to avoid 'looking into our gift-horse's mouth with a magnifying glass', before adding that 'Estella surely cannot be a condition of' Pip's 'inheritance' (246). He also warns Pip that his pursuit of Estella 'may lead to miserable things' (246). Pip insists that it is 'impossible' to 'detach' himself from Estella. It seems as if the narrator has brainwashed himself that fate or fortune has decreed that they should be together.

Pip's close relationship with Herbert is further highlighted by the latter sharing the news that he has a 'secret': he is engaged to Clara (248). Herbert seems even more foolish than Pip, in regards to money, as when asked what Clara's father lives on, Herbert replies: 'On the first floor' (249). While injecting humour into the dialogue, the writer has successfully conveyed the idea that Herbert is just as incurably romantic and unrealistic as Pip.

The motif of shaking hands appears at the end of the chapter, as the pair 'warmly' shake upon their 'mutual confidence' before heading off into the night to see Wopsle acting in Shakespeare's 'Hamlet' (250).

Chapter 31

Like Hamlet, Pip is haunted by ghosts of the past and is searching for his identity through a list father, so Wopsle's play is very apt. Imagery of rottenness and decay pervades both 'Hamlet' and 'Great Expectations', and there is even 'a noble boy in the wash-leather boots of a gigantic ancestor' in this version, which is somewhat reminiscent of the 'Avenger' (250). The grief-stricken Orphelia, meanwhile, can be likened to Miss Havisham, when she shakes off 'her white muslin scarf', before folding it and burying it (251).

Pip cannot help but laugh 'from ear to ear' at Wopsle's performance as 'that undecided Prince', despite 'Hamlet' being a tragedy (252, 251, 252). Although he is 'afraid' to say 'a word about the play', Pip and Herbert are 'not quick enough' to leave at the end of the performance without meeting Wopsle first (253, 252). Therefore, they are asked their opinion and Pip simply echoes Herbert's platitudes, such as 'massive and concrete' when asked by Mr Waldengarver (also known as Wopsle) to comment on his 'reading of the character' (254). The narrator switches between Wopsle's real name and his stage name, making him into a bizarre gothic double of himself. In this way, Wopsle is similar to Pip, who also has an alter ego, being known as Handel by Herbert.

Feeling sorry for Wopsle, Pip and Herbert take him out for supper. Like Pip, Wopsle is self-indulgent, 'reviewing his success and developing his plans' until two in the morning (255). Both have great expectations and both have been ridiculed: Pip by Trabb's boy and Wopsle by his theatre audience.

Chapter 32

Rising tension and mystery marks the start of this chapter, as we don't know who has written to Pip, who confesses he has 'never seen the handwriting' before (255). However, by the end of the letter, we discover that the mystery writer is none other than Estella. Pip's reaction is typical of someone who is totally infatuated, as he admits: 'My appetite vanished instantly' (256).

On the way to meet Estella, Pip bumps into Wemmick, who has sympathy for a client, who has been 'accused' (256). He makes it clear that something like that could happen to anyone, by saying: 'Either of us might be accused of it, you know' (256). Pip's reply is harsh: 'Only neither of us is' (256).

Wemmick seems to think Pip needs educating, so takes him to Newgate Prison. Wemmick displays a professional detachment, judging by the writer's analogy that he 'walked among the prisoners, much as a gardener might walk among his plants' (257). The same imagery continues as they walk through 'Wemmick's greenhouse', which could imply there is no escape for these plants, whose crimes are there to be seen (258).

After talking to the Colonel, it appears that Wemmick will receive 'a pair of pigeons', which he regards as 'portable property' (259). Wemmick is much more approachable than Jaggers, but that only makes Pip more 'impressed' by his guardian's 'subtlety' (260). However, Pip wishes he had a guardian with 'minor abilities' instead, as like everyone else, he is intimidated by Jaggers (260).

The chapter closes with Pip thinking 'with absolute abhorrence of the contrast between the jail and' Estella (261). Later, when we find out more about her ancestry, we will consider Pip's thoughts to be ironic.

Chapter 33

Pip is still just as much, if not more, enamoured with Estella, as he reveals that she 'seemed more delicately beautiful than she had ever seemed yet' (261). She is quite regimented, insisting she that he and she 'obey [...] instructions' (261). She is heading for 'Surrey Richmond', which implies she is will be becoming even richer (261).

In keeping with the idea of gothic doubles, Pip points out that Estella speaks of herself as if she 'were some one else' (262). That distant way about her may cause her to 'burst out laughing' at Pip, which makes her seem cruel and spiteful (263). She explains how she laughs when people 'fail' and how she gains 'satisfaction' from seeing 'those people thwarted' (263, 264).

As they journey together, Pip admits he to himself how 'ashamed' he is that he know Newgate, which makes Estellla respond with the word: 'Wretches' (265). She is almost as dismissive about Jaggers's home, which she speculates must be 'a curious place' (266).

Finally, she refers to 'Pip' by name and this 'was the first time' (267). She seems to be treating him as an equal at last.

When he returns to Hammersmith, Mrs Pocket had lost some 'needles', which doesn't augur well with some many young one around (268). Perhaps, it suggests that Pip's dreams of bliss will be punctured.

Chapter 34

This bridging chapter summarises a period of moral decline in Pip's life and the guilt he feels about his treatment of Joe and Buddy. As the narrator admits: 'I lived in a state of chronic uneasiness respecting my behaviour to Joe' (268). He adds: 'My conscience was not by any means comfortable about Biddy' (268). His guilt even spreads as far as Herbert, as the narrator believes his 'influence' on others is 'not beneficial' to them (269). Pip appears to be extremely self-absorbed and, despite his guilt, has not yet formed a plan of action which will set matters right.

His obsession with Estella continues, as the narrator admits he 'haunted Richmond' (270). The verb employed suggests that nothing good will come of this unhealthy preoccupation with a heartless girl. However, Pip's inability to treat his friends properly might make him a good match for her. Perhaps she is all he deserves for his poor behaviour, which even turns violent when he 'went so far as to seize the Avenger by his blue collar', making him airborne 'like a booted Cupid' (271). Actually, the Avenger is

Pip's creation, as he and Herbert get more 'more into debt', the narrator's patience wears thin and his frustration mounts.

Pip and Herbert try to sort out their financial affairs, ironically by buying 'plenty of stationery' (272). The narrator's inflated ego is apparent, as he admits he feels 'like a bank of some sort, rather than a private individual' (273).

As well facing up to debts, Pip may be sobered by the thought of attending his sister's 'internment' (274). He receives the news of the death from Trabb and Co, and the narrator does not comment upon his feelings regarding the news. We can only assume he remains business-like and more focused on his debt, given that lack of love between him and Mrs Joe.

Chapter 35

This chapter contains a mixture of pathos and satire. It begins with the narrator initially describing 'the gap' left by his sister dying as being 'wonderful' (274). However, this joyful emotion is tempered with 'a violent indignation against the assailant from whom she had suffered so much' (274). He goes on to name Orlick and it either shows that blood is thicker than water or that Pip's hatred for his previous work colleague outstrips his anger at his sister. This anger seems to dissipate as he remembers his sister 'with a gentle tone', which even softens 'the edge of Tickler' (275).

The funeral turns out to be bogusly theatrical and crudely ostentatious, with Trabb insisting that they all get their 'pocket-handkerchiefs out' (276). The 'larks' singing as she is laid to rest in the churchyard reminds the reader of Joe's reference to larks as another word for laughs.

Pip takes the opportunity to admonish Biddy for not informing him of the news, but he does not persist as he doesn't want to make her cry. Biddy's future is unclear, but she interrupts Pip when tries to mention money. Her reply to Pip's half-finished sentence: 'If you want any mo---' shows how proud she is (279).

When she tells Pip about his sister's final moments, she cries and the narrator comments that 'the stars that were coming out, were blurred in my own sight' (280). It could mean that Pip is crying too or that his obsession with Estella (symbolised by stars) is lessened by being in the presence of another love interest: Biddy. However, Estella remains at the top of the pecking order being 'under the stars with a clear and honest eye' (281).

Chapter 36

Pip is celebrating his twenty-first birthday, his coming of age, which is particularly important in a Bildungsroman novel. Congratulating him, we discover that Jaggers is 'a remarkably short shaker' of hands, which tells us the lawyer does not really care about people that much; Pip is a professional assignment to him, nothing more.

As well as the hand shaking, another motif is 'the two ghostly casts' and, likewise, they also do not augur well for Pip's prospects. Jaggers asks Pip to confirm that he is 'in debt' (283). However, he gives Pip 'five hundred pounds' and tells him that from now on he will be able to draw 'one hundred and twenty-five pounds per quarter' until he is 'communication with the fountainhead' or, in other words, his benefactor (284). Perhaps the implication here is Pip has been spending money like water.

Pip wants to know more about when his benefactor will reveal himself, but almost gets more reaction out of 'the two horrible casts of the twitched faces' which 'looked [...] as if they had come to a crisis in their suspended attention, and were going to sneeze' (285). In the absence of facts, Pip is free to speculate wildly about 'the notion that Miss Havisham [...] had not taken him [Jaggers] into her confidence as to her designing me for Estella' (286). Pip has assumed a lot from very little.

Nevertheless, despite his guardian's reticence, Pip invites Jaggers to 'dine' with him, which implies the narrator has a generous nature (286). The narrative continues in that vein, as Pip asks Wemmick advice about helping a 'friend' to 'get on. In commercial life' (287). Wemmick replies that Pip might just as well 'pitch' his 'money into the Thames over the centre arch' of a bridge (287). This analogy is 'very discouraging' for Pip, who wants to put the windfall to good use and, at least, appears to morally on the mend (287).

However, Wemmick says Pip is 'welcome' to come to Walworth 'in a private and personal capacity' to discuss the issue again (288). Wemmick's advice is so much more wholesome than Jaggers, who doesn't have 'an Aged [...] or a Stinger [...] to unbend his brows' (288). Jaggers simply makes Pip and Herbert feel 'intensely melancholy' (288). Unlike Wemmick, there is no personal side to Jaggers, who remains professionally distant at all times.

Chapter 37

Wemmick's home or 'Castle' is a cosy, domestic idyll, away from all the legal entanglements of his professional life (288). It is an apt setting for Pip's unselfish attempt to do something morally good, hence his 'pilgrimage' there (288).

He is met by the Aged, who is extremely 'hard of hearing' (289). This adds humour to this section as Pip has to speak loudly, while it also reminds us that everyone needs a home where they do not have to listen to the problems of the world; the Aged is doubly cut off in that he is: in the 'Castle' and also deaf.

We meet Miss Skiffins, who is described as having 'a wooden appearance' (290). She and John Wemmick make a homely couple, as the verb that is repeated, 'tumbled', is reminiscent of the word used to describe the children of the Pockets and their chaotic, domestic bliss (290).

When Wemmick suggests a 'walk' around 'the property', Pip takes the opportunity to confide in Wemmick on the already mentioned intention to reward Herbert for his help, as if he had 'never hinted at it before' (291). This shows how the domestic Wemmick appears to be nothing like the professional legal clerk that he is with Jaggers.

Wemmick says he'll contact Skiffins's brother, who is 'an accountant and agent' (292). It is beginning to look as if Pip will get the help he requires to do something 'devilish good' (292). It implies that there is something tainted about the money Pip wants to give Herbert but, at this stage, we are none the wiser about what that might be.

The kindness and patience of Wemmick is mentioned explicitly in the text, when he allows the Aged to 'tip' the paper (293). While the Aged reads aloud, Wemmick is 'untiring and gentle in his vigilance' (293). This proves what a caring man Wemmick is.

Meanwhile, the prudish morality of the time is revealed by 'Wemmick's arm beginning to disappear', as he makes advances towards Miss Skiffins (294). She stops these advances with 'the neatness of a placid boxer' (294). It all appears to be part of the entertainment for Pip and the reader, alike.

The upshot of this visit to the Castle is that Miss Skiffins's brother conducts 'the negotiation' and 'the whole business' is 'so cleverly managed, that Herbert' has 'not the least suspicion' of Pip's 'hand being in it' (295). This links the hand-shaking motif, and shows how the suddenly unselfish Pip has finally accomplished something he can be proud of on his journey to becoming a kind, beneficent gentleman.

Chapter 38

The gothic genre is never far from the text as here the narrator reveals that if the 'staid old house near the Green at Richmond' ever becomes 'haunted', the it will be haunted by him and his 'unquiet spirit' (295, 296). We get a sense that Pip has an unhealthy obsession with the place and, more particularly, its occupant, Estella. He even mentions her 'cold careless smiles that always chilled' him (297). The alliteration adds to the sense that the narrator is attracted by her poise and beauty, although horrified at her lack of warmth.

Nevertheless, Estella wants to pay Pip to escort her to Satis House, where there 'no change', unsurprisingly (298) Pip still misreads the situation, thinking that 'the prize' or Estella was 'reserved' for him (298, 299). 'Reserved' works as a pun here, as Estella is reluctant to reveal her feelings, if she has any.

Even Miss Havisham accuses Estella of possessing a 'cold, cold heart' (300). Miss Havisham compares that to her 'burning love' for Estella. This phrase foreshadows Miss Havisham's fate.

Miss Havisham also complains about how Estella is 'so proud, so proud' (301). The repetition helps to highlight Miss Havisham's disappointment.

This infects Pip too, as 'with a depressed heart' he walks 'in the starlight', which is a reference to Estella and he even dreams about: 'A thousand Miss Havishams, who 'haunted' him (302, 303).

Pip is also haunted by the very real spectre of Drummle courting Estella, which the narrator becomes aware of when the latter calls 'upon the company to pledge him to' the aforementioned lady (304). Pip is incensed, but knows 'The Spider' is a formidable for (305). Like a spider, Drummle is ready to wait his chance. This image links to cobwebs at Satis House.

Estella won't take responsibility for Drummle's attentions, saying: 'moths, and all sorts of ugly creatures [...] hover about a lighted candle. Can the candle help it?' (307) The rhetorical question makes her seem slightly more palatable as a character and, therefore, more of a suitable love match for Pip.

However, the idea of Drummle, 'the boor', and Estella being romantically linked makes Pip 'wretched' (307). The use of emotive language makes us understand the full force of his revulsion. She tells him to not to be 'foolish' (307).

Pip cannot help but feel like 'in the Eastern story', when 'the ceiling fell' (308). In effect, the narrator's world has crashed in.

Chapter 39

Given the nature of a Bildungsroman novel, perhaps it is no surprise that at the age of 'three-and-twenty', Pip has moved to Temple, in London (308). This real setting is forever associated with the Knights Templar, who were famous for their initiation ceremonies. Pip has been initiated, likewise, into the world of gentlemen, complete with debts, theatrical entertainment and 'reading' (308).

The mood becomes increasing gothic, in the stormy winter setting, with tension and suspense created through sound imagery, such as: 'I heard a footstep on the stair' (309). We gradually discover that the owner of the footstep wants to see Pip and is 'substantially dressed, but roughly; like a voyager by sea' (310). We find out that this man with 'a face' that is 'strange' to Pip is 'about sixty' years old, with 'long iron grey hair' (310). This is similar to Magwitch's description in chapter one: 'A fearful man, all in coarse grey, with a great iron on his leg' (4).

Due to the clues in the narrative, the reader may guess before Pip that the 'strange' man is indeed the convict, Magwitch, whose name has still not been revealed yet. The narrator states: 'I could not have known my convict more distinctly than I knew him now' (311). Using the possessive pronoun, 'my', makes Pip's connection to Magwitch seems almost familial.

However, now that he's a gentleman, Pip is aloof and stand-offish with Magwitch, evidenced when he says: 'I cannot wish to renew that chance intercourse with you of long ago, under these different circumstances' (312). Pip regrets that he has spoken 'harshly' to the convict, seeing that Magwitch's 'eyes were full of tears' (313). This shows that Pip quickly reflects on his own behaviour and is slowly maturing into a more moral gentleman. He tries to do the right thing by 'pay back' Magwitch back the 'two one-pound notes', which were given to Pip earlier in the narrative (313-314).

Magwitch promptly burns them in the 'lamp' and the light imagery may reflect the idea that dark secrets will soon be illuminated for both Pip and the reader (314). Pip reacts melodramatically to the news that Magwitch has 'made a gentleman' out of him, when he reports that he feels like he is 'suffocating' (315). Pip recoils from Magwitch's 'touch as if he had been a snake', although the latter refers to himself as the former's 'second father' (316, 315). Clearly, Pip feels shocked, disgusted and ungrateful.

Like Miss Havisham, Magwitch is proud of his creation but, unlike her, he has not noticed that Pip has not returned his love. This is clearly shown, when Magwitch lays his hand on Pip's 'shoulder' and the narrator reports that: 'I shuddered at the thought that for anything I knew, his hand might be stained with blood' (317).

Pip seems shocked at his own 'repugnance' but is ready to take on responsibility for hiding Magwitch from the authorities. Magwitch was sent to a penal colony in Australia (where he made Pip's fortune), but 'it's death to come back' to Britain as he was sentenced 'for life' (318).

Pip allows Magwitch to stay in Herbert's room, while reflecting using apt nautical imagery (given the convict's lengthy sea voyages) about 'how wrecked' he is (319). Pip's imagination is running wild as he imagines he hears 'pursuers' in the stormy night and lacks logic in his assumption that 'it might not be safe to be shut up there with him in the dead of the wild solitary night' (319). Pip seems to have quickly forgotten how affectionately Magwitch has looked upon him and how generously he has paid out to allow the former to become a gentleman. Consequently, Pip locks Magwitch in the bedroom while reflecting again on his 'perception' of his own 'wretchedness' (320). The word 'perception' implies that the maturer Pip may have decided in hindsight that there was no 'wretchedness' to complain of really.

Chapter 40

Part three of the novel begins more positively, as Pip admits it was 'fortunate' for that he 'had to take precautions to ensure [...] the safety of' his 'dreaded visitor' (323). The pressing need to keep Magwitch safe is stopping Pip from becoming too self-indulgent.

Meanwhile, the tension rises quickly as Pip trips over 'a man crouching in a corner' of 'the black staircase'. We do not know who this lurking man is, which adds suspense and a bit of horror, given that he is enveloped in darkness. The night watchman can only tell Pip that the 'lurker' had 'a dust-coloured kind of clothes on, under a dark coat'. The writer uses free indirect speech to quickly convey the idea that the lurker's presence is ominous.

Reminiscent of the metallic quality of Magwitch's 'iron grey hair', the next morning is 'all of a leaden hue' (310, 325). At this point, Pip and the readers finally discover Magwitch's name and that he was brought up to be 'a warmint' (326). As this word is a variant of vermin, Magwitch is describing himself in animalistic terms. The narrator follows suit by comparing him to 'a hungry old dog' (327).

Despite the narrator's lurid portrait of Magwitch, the convict's concern about not wanting to be 'low' implies he is a more complex character than Pip initially thinks (328). His bravery is evident, when he refers to himself as an 'old bird' who is 'not afeerd to perch upon a scarecrow' (329). The bird imagery could symbolise the freedom from abject poverty that Magwitch has bought Pip. In a sense, Magwitch has bought the metaphorical wings of a gentleman that Pip needs to keep airborne.

Pip decides he will pretend Magwitch is his uncle and resolves to call him 'Mr Provis' (330). Perhaps that name is a play on the word 'provisional', as Pip may expect this to be a temporary state of affairs. It also connects with the word 'provide' and, in that respect, it links to Magwitch's role as Pip's secret benefactor. This role is confirmed by Jaggers, who informs the narrator that it is 'only' Magwitch who has provided the means to allow Pip to enjoy a gentleman's lifestyle (331). The narrator admits he is 'downcast' about the revelation, as he always assumed it was Miss Havisham (332).

Jaggers warns Pip to 'take nothing on looks' and 'the two vile casts on the shelf' seem to echo the sentiment that the lawyer is always right (333).

Meanwhile, Magwitch is like Joe in that Pip's attempts to dress him better fail 'dismally' (333). This ties together the two father figures in Pip's life; in some ways, the narrator is ashamed of them both and seems ungrateful for their huge contributions to his life chances.

Magwitch is fearsome in Pip's eyes, which is evidenced when the narrator states: 'I doubt if a ghost could have been more terrible to me'. It seems as if Pip wants to sever all ties with the past. The horror Pip sees in this 'misshapen creature' is reminiscent of Frankenstein's feeling towards his creation in Mary Shelley's novel (335). Ironically, it is Magwitch who has made Pip, rather than the other way around.

At this point, Herbert appears, addressing Pip as 'Handel' as is his custom, and is sworn to secrecy by Magwitch, who makes him 'kiss' his 'little clasped black book' (335). We assume this must be the Bible, as Magwitch adds: 'Lord strike you dead on the spot, if ever you split in any way sumever' (336). This foreshadows court scenes and the swearing of legal oaths set to appear later in the narrative.

Chapter 41

The writer informs us of the 'astonishment and disquiet of Herbert' regarding Pip's telling of 'the whole of the secret' in reported speech (336). This necessarily speeds up the narrative, as the reader and Pip already know this information.

Magwitch refers to himself as 'muzzled', which combines dog imagery with the idea that he lacks freedom of speech in his current predicament (337).

However, Magwitch 'is intent upon various new expenses', which alarms Pip (338). The narrator is feeling very self-absorbed, calling himself 'fit for nothing' (338). He mentions he could become 'a soldier', but then he breaks down, which implies he is just being melodramatic and is too mentally weak for the aforementioned profession (338).

Pip's hyperbole knows no bounds in this section, as he claims he 'would far far rather have worked at the forge all the days' of his life than 'come to this!' (339). The exclamation mark adds to the idea that Pip's reaction to Magwitch's arrival is quite immature.

The motif of handshaking recurs as Pip and Herbert 'shake hands upon' the idea of getting Magwitch out of England (340). This reminds us how close the pair have become.

The chapter ends with the introduction of a story within a story, as Magwitch turns 'an angry eye on the fire' before relating the tale of the other convict that Pip saw him 'struggle' with 'on the marshes' (341). Magwitch looking at the fire makes it seem as if he is taking inspiration from hell, in order to tell the story.

Chapter 42

Magwitch's embedded narrative fills in the gaps in Pip's story so far, so is very important to the reader. The convict repeats the phrase 'in jail and out of jail' to convey the idea that his life was quite unremarkable initially (342).

We then are told of the name 'Compeyson' for the first time. Perhaps this could connote compost or competition, although this arch-villain is described as 'good-looking' as well as a smooth-talking, learned gentleman (343). In that sense, he is hardly the archetypal Victorian antagonist.

Magwitch says Compeyson had 'no more heart than an iron file', which reminds us of how Pip stole an instrument of that nature from Joe and how it was used to free the convict from his leg iron (344).

Compeyson is referred to as a 'coward' and his wife and Magwitch have to deal with ravings of his dying friend, Arthur (345).

The injustice of that plus what happens 'in the dock' makes us realise that Compeyson is irresponsible and unkind (346). Looking like a gentleman with 'his curly hair and his black clothes and his white pocket-handkerchief' means the court is ready to blame all misdemeanours on the 'wretch' that is Magwitch (346). Interestingly, Pip has been describing himself repeatedly as wretched earlier, so this links the two characters.

Magwitch relates how Compeyson gets 'seven year', while he gets double that amount for the crimes they've commuted (347). This highlights how unfair the criminal justice system was, as a gentleman would be likely to receive a lesser punishment than someone as low as Magwitch.

While Magwitch is telling his tale, Herbert writes a secret note to Pip, which tells him: 'Compeyson is the man who professed to be Miss Havisham's lover' (348). When they look at Magwitch he is 'smoking by the fire', which foreshadows the fate of one of the main characters (349).

Chapter 43

A rhetorical question offers the reader food for thought at the opening of the chapter as the narrator wonders: 'Why should I pause to ask how much of my shrinking from Provis might be traced to Estella?' (349). This comment is ironic given the revelation that happens later in the novel. At this stage, Pip believes there is an 'abyss' between his beloved Estella and the loathed Magwitch (349). This shows how misguided Pip is by his own delusions of grandeur.

His love of Estella causes Pip to venture out 'like a beggar' towards Miss Havisham's (350). This shows that Pip still has an inferiority complex. On the way, he meets the 'poisonous' Bentley Drummle and the pair pretend not to see each other (350). In some respects, Pip is bringing himself down to Drummle's level with this behaviour.

Pip's competitive and jealous behaviour makes it seem as if Trabb's boy was right to copy him with 'Don't know yah' comments, earlier in the narrative. When he wants to stir the fire in the coffee-room of the Blue Boar, Pip has to put his hand behind Drummle's 'legs for the poker' (351). Even then, Pip pretends 'not to know him' (351).

The pair trade insults: Drummle claiming that this area is a 'beastly place', while Pip compares it to the latter's 'Shropshire' (351). Drummle seems to have the upper hand though, as he will be meeting Estella and consequently he has 'an insolent triumph on his great-jowled face' (352). Pip is 'cut' to the 'heart' by this, and seems to realise he must admit defeat judging by the word 'triumph' being attributed to Drummle's face. That victory is symbolised by Drummle taking 'a cigar from his pocket' and biting the end off, as if in celebration that he has won the race for Estella (353). The narrator merges his antagonist's together by remarking that 'the slouched shoulders' and the 'ragged hair of this man' reminds him 'of Orlick' (353). This highlights how much Pip hates their pair, while also emphasising how possessive, given his anger towards anyone who pursues his two love interests: Estella and Biddy.

Chapter 44

The setting in Miss Havisham's room is unmistakably gothic with 'wax candles' burning 'on the wall', perhaps evoking a feeling that there would be a eerie glow and shadows being cast around the room (354). However, the focus is on Estella 'knitting' (354). This makes her appear domesticated, passive and very much the archetypal ideal Victorian woman.

By contrast, Miss Havisham responds fiercely when Pip asks her if it was 'kind' of her to allow him to go on believing she was his benefactor. She strikes 'her stick upon the floor [...] so suddenly' that even Estella glances up 'in surprise' (355). Miss Havisham insists that Pip 'made' his own 'snares' and disclaims any responsibility (356).

However, the more mature Pip has become more unselfish. He shows moral strength to put his friend's interests ahead of his own asking Miss Havisham if she 'would spare the money to do' his 'friend Herbert a lasting service in life' (357).

When Pip returns to the subject of his love of Estella, the latter is as icy as Hans Christian Anderson's 'Snow Queen'. Although it may be unnatural to be so cold, Estella states: 'It is in my nature' (358).

It seems that Pip has invested in an idealised version of Estella as the completion of his own new identity. It was always an adolescent fantasy doomed to failure, but at least she won't be 'a blessing' to Drummle (359). Of that, she assures him.

Watching all the drama unfolding is the 'spectral figure of Miss Havisham', with 'her hand still covering her heart' (360). She feels a mixture of 'pity and remorse', the narrator believes (360). Perhaps she really does have a soft spot for Pip, or perhaps he is deluding himself, as she created Estella to break hearts.

The chapter ends on a cliffhanger at 'past midnight' as Wemmick leaves a note with the night-porter, which reads: 'DON'T GO HOME' (361). The capital letters and device of the note make it seem all the more important that Pip follows the advice. The reader is left wondering where Pip will go next.

Chapter 45

Pip heads for 'the Hummums in Covent Garden', which is another gothic destination given its 'vault on the ground floor' (361). His room has 'a despotic monster of a four-post bedstead in it', which adds to eerie nature of the place (362).

The critic Steven Connor suggests that Pip is caught up by this sudden inexplicable twist of fate, which now makes him almost endlessly 'conjugate' the 'vast shadowy verb' of 'Don't go home' (363).

Pip goes to see Wemmick and is given long-winded clues as to what has been going on in his absence. Wemmick refrains from being more direct as he says: 'it's as well not to mention names when avoidable' (364). For the reader, it certainly adds suspense. He adds that he won't 'go into' who is watching Pip's quarters in 'Garden-court, Temple' (365). Nevertheless, Pip thanks him for his 'valuable advice' (366).

Wemmick also relates that Herbert has removed 'Tom, Jack, or Richard' (or Magwitch, in other words) to somewhere safer: 'by the river-side' (367). The grateful Pip is not slow in 'shaking' hands with Wemmick, as the symbolic motif recurs again.

The chapter ends with a break from the drama, as Pip enjoys the company of the Aged by 'falling asleep before' the fire (369). Here, the hearth offers domestic bliss and comfort to Pip, who needs to recover his energy before the travails that lie ahead.

Chapter 46

The setting here evokes the mood of chapter one, with its prison hulks in the Medway. The narrator mentions the 'ooze and slime and other dregs of the tide' in this waterside scene, which makes it seem like it could be a hotbed of criminal activity or worse (369).

As he gets closer to where Magwitch is holed up, the narrative uses nautical imagery to make the scene seem more appropriate for an escaped convict, who has illegally returned from exile in Australia. The 'shells upon the chimney piece' and 'the coloured engravings on the wall, representing the death of Captain Cook' seem particularly apt, given that the latter was famous for charting Australia (370).

We hear more about the love of Herbert's life, Miss Clara Barley, now that Magwitch is housed there as 'an upper lodger' (371). We discover, she has 'no mother', which makes her similar to Pip and Estella (371). Herbert reefers to her father, meanwhile, as 'old Gruffandgrim' (371). Pip agrees that old Barley is a 'truculent Ogre' to his 'captive fairy' daughter, Clara (371). Their relationship can be compared unfavourably with Wemmick's with the Aged. The close juxtaposition of the two accounts makes 'poor Clara's supper' seem all the more meagre (372). We discover that old Bill Barley 'would commune with himself by the day and night', which gives the impression that Clara is supervising a mental asylum for one (373). This all works to make a Clara a sympathetic character for the reader.

Meanwhile, Pip and Herbert 'scheme' about how to transport Magwitch somewhere even safer, much to the latter's delight (374). We discover that Herbert has invented a third false name for Magwitch: 'Campbell' to keep him safe (375).

The chapter ends with a cliffhanger, as the narrator reveals how he views the Thames 'with dread' in that it flows downstream towards Magwitch and 'that any black mark on its surface might be his pursuers, going swiftly, silently, and surely, to take him' (376). The triplet with sibilants works here to make the 'pursuers' appear snake-like and sly.

Chapter 47

The chapter begins by telling us that 'weeks passed', which allows time to pass quickly without wasting time on conveying details (376).

The personification of Pip's 'worldly affairs' which 'wear a gloomy appearance' make them seem so much worse to the reader (377). This bleak outlook is matched by the bleak setting that follows as we expect a setback, once we are told it is a 'raw evening' in February (378). It is reminiscent of the weather when Pip first encounters Magwitch.

In the depths of despair, Pip seeks out some light entertainment by visiting Wopsle's theatre. In this farcical account of the performance, we are told how 'Mr Wopsle (who had never been heard of before)' is 'coming in with a star and garter on' (379). Although Wopsle is playing a 'plenipotentiary of great power', he only has a bit part in the production (379). Hence, Wopsle's declining fortunes seem to mirror Pip's, which reminds the reader how miserable the narrator must be in his current predicament.

The irony of the stage performance is there is more going on off-stage than on it, as Wopsle asks Pip after the show: 'who else was there?' (380). This adds tension, as we already know Pip is being followed. The writer makes the idea more gothic and frightening by saying to Pip: 'you were quite unconscious of him, sitting behind you, like a ghost' (381). Eventually, we find out it was Compeyson, as Wopsle tells Pip it was 'one of the two prisoners' who was 'sat behind you' (381).

Adding to the gothic fear already created, the writer uses reported speech to relate that Compeyson was dressed 'prosperously [...] in black' (382). Usually, that colour symbolises death and is considered ominous.

The word 'cautious' is repeated, at the end of the chapter, to emphasise how little Pip can do to change the situation. He can only be careful and nothing more, at this stage.

Chapter 48

We discover how Jaggers has slipped in Pip's estimation as the latter almost declines the former's invitation 'to dine' (383). In the end, Pip accepts because 'Wemmick's coming' (383).

Some images of death are presented to us, while Pip waits in Jaggers's office, with 'candle-snuffing', 'dirty winding-sheets' and the reappearance of 'the two casts' making the scene particularly gothic (384).

When all three go to Gerrard-street, Wemmick is like the 'wrong' twin of himself (384). In a sense, he is like his own gothic double.

After passing on a message that Pip is to go to Miss Havisham's, Jaggers makes a toast to Drummle, who 'has played his cards [...] and won the pool' (385). It seems that Pip's luck has run out. However, Jaggers believes Drummle might 'beat' up Estella (his future wife), foreshadowing the prospect of domestic violence (385).

For the first time, Pip notices a similarity between Jaggers's servant, Molly, and Estella, who was portrayed knitting in a previous scene. Here Molly's 'action of her fingers' is compared to 'like the action of knitting' (386). He feels sure 'this woman' is 'Estella's mother' (386). In some ways, Pip's guess is a bit of a quantum leap but, bearing in mind Jaggers's connection with Miss Havisham, the idea does have some traction, despite the mistakes the narrator made about the identity of his own benefactor.

Once Wemmick leaves with Pip, he can be his other self once more. The lawyer's clerk admits: 'I feel I have to screw myself up when I dine with him [Jaggers] - and I dine more comfortably unscrewed' (387). This seems to indicate how stressful and unnatural it is for Wemmick to be with Jaggers after working hours.

Pip takes the opportunity to ask about Molly, and is told that she has 'some gypsy blood' (388). In the nineteenth century, this would normally be taken to mean that she had a passionate nature, especially as she had been tried for 'jealousy' (388). In this regard, she is completely opposite to the cold, calculating Estella.

Wemmick relates how there were suspicions that Molly 'frantically destroyed her child' by the man who wronged her (390). This child was 'said to have been a girl' (390). This revelation seems to indicate that Pip is right and Estella is Molly's child.

Chapter 49

As Pip embarks on his trip to Miss Havisham's, the setting is gothic and gloomy, with the 'cathedral chimes' having 'a sadder and more remote sound' than usual (390).

Upon reaching Satis House, it is obvious that the newly mature Pip has a more forgiving nature than his predecessor, as he stands 'compassionating' Miss Havisham (391). It appears he will get his just reward, which is 'nine hundred pounds' to secretly help Herbert, if he will keep her 'secret' (392). This secrecy adds to the gothic flavour of the novel.

Miss Havisham then asks Pip to write: 'I forgive her' under her name (393). However, Pip admits that he wants 'forgiveness' too (393). It seems as if he is on the way to redeeming himself and learning from the error of his previously selfish ways, a bit like Scrooge in 'A Christmas Carol' (393).

Miss Havisham, likewise, feels so much guilt, which is evident in the way 'she wrung her hands, and crushed her white hair' (394). She admits she was instrumental in turning Estella into an 'Ice Queen', by stealing 'her heart away' and putting 'ice in its place' (395). It appears that the writer believes environmental factors affect an individual's development more than genes.

The light is dying, like Miss Havisham appears to be, when Pip leaves with 'twilight [...] closing in' (396). Pip's hopes have decayed like Miss Havisham and the 'growth of fungus' that he passes through on his way out emphasise that (396-397).

However, Pip's moral regeneration continues with his brave attempt to save Miss Havisham, who is consumed by 'a whirl of fire blazing all about her' (397). He holds her down 'like a prisoner who might escape' but it is all in vain (397). She is going to pay the ultimate price for her sins: death. Meanwhile, fire is purgatorial and painful here for Pip, who burns 'both' hands (398). This fire is nothing like a reassuring hearth or the forge's furnace.

Although dying, Miss Havisham continually asks for Pip's forgiveness, which he grants the next morning at 'six o'clock' with a kiss on the 'lips' and with the words that she requested (399).

Chapter 50

When he is reflecting almost religiously, it seems entirely appropriate that Pip should be located in Temple, in the 'chambers' he shares with Herbert (399). Pip recollects the 'flames' (399).

Herbert is caring for Pip, removing his bandages, while asking him if he'd like to know more about Magwitch's 'woman that he had great trouble with' (400). This introduction to the story increases the suspense.

We discover that the woman is Molly, as we are told she was 'jealous' and was 'defended' by Jaggers (401). While telling Magwitch's story, Herbert uses the former's mannerism, calling Pip 'dear boy' (402). This makes the account appear more realistic.

The last words of the chapter are Pip's, as he reveals to Herbert that 'the man' they have 'in hiding down the river, is Estella's father' (403). This works as an effective cliffhanger, as we wonder how everyone concerned will react to this news, if indeed it is broken.

Chapter 51

After the revelation that the pure and distant Estella is inextricably linked to crime through her father, Magwitch, Pip admits he is guilty of wishful thinking when he says that perhaps: 'I was glad to transfer to the man in whose preservation I was so much concerned, some rays of romantic interest' (403). Pip may be relieved that she is tainted by association and, consequently, he feels a stronger connection with her.

When Pip described Miss Havisham's end to Jaggers, the latter resembles Satan, as he stands 'according to his wont, before the fire' (404). Nevertheless, Pip's comment that he knows 'more of Estella's history than even' Jaggers does brings the lawyer to 'an indefinably attentive stop' (405). When Pip finally reveals that Magwitch is her father, 'even Mr Jaggers started' (406). This episode marks a turning point for Pip, as this is the first time he has shocked the un-shockable lawyer.

The revelations continue, as Pip turns to Wemmick and says: 'I know you to be a man with a gentle heart. I have seen your pleasant home, and your old father' (407). This also shocks Jaggers to the core, bringing about more honesty between the two legal professionals and a sea change in their relationship.

Jaggers agrees to tell Pip 'all', about Estella, whom he describes as 'one pretty child out of the heap, who could be saved; whom the father believed dead, and [...] over the mother, the legal adviser had this power' (408). As usual, Jaggers still remains circumspect, and careful not to incriminate himself, insisting that he makes 'no admissions' (409).

Business continues as normal, when their attentions turn to Mike, whom Wemmick describes as 'spluttering like a bad pen' (410). This simile shows that Mike is not functioning properly, while reminding the reader that the legal profession is all about paperwork. This interlude reestablishes Jaggers's and Wemmick's 'good understanding' (411).

Chapter 52

Herbert is almost a gothic double of a younger Pip, with his romantic notions 'of himself conducting Clara Barkley to the land of the Arabian Nights' and of Pip 'going out to join them (with a caravan of camels...) (411). Now that Pip has matured, his imagination is not quite as vivid as Herbert's, who has not been changed in the same way by bitter experience. The alliterative 'c's reminds us that Herbert longs to travel with the love of his life. By contrast, Pip has been spurned by Estella.

The plot picks up pace again, following a written message from Wemmick, which Pip must 'burn' after reading (412). The added secrecy adds tension, while the word 'burn' reminds of that dramatic demise of Miss Havisham and of the danger that could be involved in this enterprise.

Another letter adds more mystery to the narrative, as Pip receives an invitation to go to the 'old marshes' and more specifically the 'old sluice-house by the limekiln' that night or the following morning to find out 'information regarding [...] Provis' (413). It seems a very ominous letter that does not augur well. The prose is reflective as the narrator considers retrospectively: 'If I had had ample time for consideration, I believe I should still have gone' (414). This line serves to increase the pace of the narrative, as Pip is up against the clock.

Once Pip arrives at the Blue Boar, he feels guilty when he hears that Pumblechook has allegedly 'done everything for him', whereas 'long-suffering and loving'Joe' and 'sweet-tempered Biddy' have 'never' complained (415). The juxtaposition of the characters makes the modest qualities of Joe and Biddy seem all the more impressive. The eating motif reappears as Pip loses his appetite as his guilt increases. The landlord notes that Pip's 'appetite's been touched' (415). The personification of an invisible force makes the guilt seem all the more powerful.

The narrator makes the juxtaposition between Joe and Pumblechook even clearer by adding: 'The falser he, the truer Joe; the meaner he, the nobler Joe' (416). The lack of a verb makes this truth seem self-evident.

Chapter 53

A typically gothic setting adds mystery and tension, as the narrative tells us: 'It was a dark night, though the full moon rose' (416). The reader may feel that something horrific is about to happen. This description is enhanced by 'the choking vapour of the kiln' which 'crept in a ghostly way' towards Pip (417). The personification adds to the idea that Pip is in grave danger.

Pip is 'caught' by someone, who is later revealed to be Orlick (418). The 'deadly look' he gives Pip reminds us of the threat he poses to the protagonist (419). The writer refers to Orlick's 'mouth snarling like a tiger', while Pip is continually called 'wolf' by the former (420). It is as if Orlick feels Pip is a pretentious gentleman and no better than an animal.

Meanwhile, Orlick refers to himself in the third person as 'Old Orlick', which suggests madness (421). That madness is fuelled by alcohol, as the narrator comments that he knew 'every drop' that Orlick's bottle 'held, was a drop of' Pip's life.

The threat of flames again is another motif, as Orlick flares 'the candle so close at' Pip, that he turns his face 'aside, to save it from the flame' (423). Structurally, this works well as it reminds the reader about Miss Havisham's death. The same may happen to Pip.

Orlick has an apt weapon to kill a former blacksmith: 'a stone-hammer' (424). However, Orlick flees and it transpires that one of the rescue team is no other that 'Trabb's boy' (425). One of the others is Herbert, who initially 'flatly refused' to tell Pip how he got there (426). He appears to be a true friend.

They return to 'Temple', which would seem to be a place of spiritual peace, given the name (427). It is a place where Pip finally begins to lose his guilt, as he admits he feels 'strong and well' (428).

Chapter 54

The 'plan' of escape for the fictional character of Magwitch was meticulously researched by Dickens, who actually chartered a boat in 1861 to take him down the Thames to Southend (429). Therefore, the author went to great lengths to achieve realism.

Through the use of personification, the writer animates the characters, as the 'crisp air, the sunlight' and 'the moving river itself' encourage Pip and his companions (430). Clearly, the narrator is worried about Magwitch, who 'the least anxious' of them (431). Perhaps the ex-convict can easily accept his fate, whatever it is. Again, Magwitch is linked to the air, which 'softened' his appearance (432). There is almost something holy or spiritual about him, as he remains 'composed and contented' (433). The alliteration draws attention to how relaxed he is.

However, the appearance of 'a melancholy gull' warns the reader that all is not well (434). It appears to be a bad omen.

Nevertheless, they make the best of their situation and even take time to come ashore in 'a dirty' public-house (435). The narrator remarks that it was probably 'not unknown to smuggling adventures' (435). This reference adds tension and excitement.

Meanwhile, the use of gothic pathetic fallacy adds to the idea that this attempt at escape is doomed. The image of the 'dismal wind [...] muttering' makes the reader recognise that Magwitch's chances of success are extremely limited (436). The danger is highlighted by 'the clouded moon', which indicates terror rather than safety (437).

We return to the recurring motif of hand shaking as the narrator reveals: 'We had all shaken hands cordially' (438). This reminds the reader of the honest and honorable nature of the protagonist and his friends.

The conflict that follows between Compeyson and Magwitch can be considered the climactic point of the novel, with the desolate estuary providing a similar backdrop to the marshes, where the first struggle took place. Structurally, the scene is cyclical for effect. The action takes place quickly and realistically, with the narrator only able to describe 'a white terror' on Compeyson's face, before both convicts disappear (439).

After the struggle, very little is made of Magwitch's 'severe injury in the chest and [...] deep cut in the head' (440). The matter-of-fact description makes Magwitch seem brave. His 'articles of dress' are in 'various stages of decay', which adds dark humour to the scene (441). Even Magwitch's old mannerism, clicking, has 'softened now', which makes the reader warm to his as character (442).

Chapter 55

This chapter provides a humorous interlude between the action scenes, as we witness Wemmick's wedding. However, before that subject is tackled, the narrator confirms that Compeyson is 'tumbling on the tides, dead' (442). It appears that Magwitch has no chance of escaping without punishment for the murder, as Jaggers reveals 'no power on earth could prevent its going against us' (443). The first-person plural 'us' reminds the reader that Pip has now invested his emotions into Magwitch, his father figure, and his fate.

The plot thickens as we discover that Herbert feels he must take 'a fine opportunity' to go to Cairo (444). The hand-shaking motif reappears as they agree that Pip will decide whether he will become 'a clerk' and join his friend in Egypt within the next 'two or three months at most' (444, 445).

Likewise, Clara will remain in England, loyally at the side of her father, Mr Barley. Pip cannot leave his own father figure until the criminal's fate is determined. Both Magwitch and Barley appear to be near death, so the reader expects both Pip and Clara to join Herbert in the Middle East soon.

Once Herbert is gone, Pip retreats to his 'lonely home - if it deserved that name' (446). One person who does have a homely place to live is Wemmick, who Pip encounters on the stairs.

The upshot is Pip is invited to Wemmick's home or 'Castle' in Walworth (447). Wemmick has metaphorically walled his worthy attributes inside his house, so the real place name is extremely appropriate. Wemmick is still hiding his forthcoming marriage from his employer, Jaggers, as we find out later in the chapter.

Wemmick repeats 'Halloa' a number of times, making the planned wedding appear spontaneous for comic effect (448). The new Mrs Wemmick then is described as 'like a violoncello in its case', finally submitting 'to be embraced as that melodious instrument might have done' (449). The musical simile makes her sound in tune with her husband and the reader expects a harmonious marriage.

Wemmick reminds Pip to be circumspect about what he has witnessed, particularly when he is around Jaggers, as the legal clerk fears his employer may think his 'brain' is 'softening' (450). It reminds the reader how it is essential to have a tough exterior to survive in London.

Chapter 56

This chapter describes Magwitch's death and, from the outset, we discover he is laying down 'in prison very ill' (450).

The court time setting is in 'April', which would remind contemporary readers of Easter and Christ's crucifixion (451). 'The drops of April rain' could be likened to tears, if we accept this is a moment of pathetic fallacy (451). A holy beam of light appears from above as the sun strikes in 'at the great windows of the court' (452). This scene appears to show Dickens's Christian morality, while offering social criticism of a system that allows a good man like Magwitch to be put to death.

After the death sentence is passed, Pip wanders the 'weary western streets of London', in a similar fashion to the writer, who often took himself out on lengthy walks of the city (453). It shows how upset Pip is by Magwitch's fate.

Pip visits Magwitch before the sentencing is carried out, and the latter says: 'I thought you was late' (454). The word late is a pun, as it also refers to someone already dead. In a sense, Magwitch is in that situation, waiting on a nineteenth-century version of Death Row.

These are Magwitch's last moments, as he passes away with the happy knowledge that his daughter, Estella, 'lived and found powerful friends' (455). The last words of the chapter: 'O Lord, be merciful to him, a sinner' are taken from the parable of the publican and the Pharisee. Its inclusion suggests that Magwitch is a humbly penitent publican, while Pip has been guilty of being a self-righteous, proud, and hypocritical Pharisee.

Chapter 57

After Magwitch's death, Pip leaves his 'chambers in the Temple' (455). It is almost as if, metaphorically, he has left his old religion (perhaps of self-indulgence) behind.

In his depressed state, he is 'arrested' for his debts (456). This mirrors the life of John Dickens, the writer's father, who was similarly profligate.

Somehow, Pip avoids arrest because of his illness and when he awakes, he finds Joe at his side. In a tender scene, we find that Joe lays 'his head down on the pillow' and puts 'his arm round' Pip's 'neck, in his joy' that the latter recognises him (457, 458). The message appears to be that you cannot be a true gentleman with being a gentle man (like Joe) first.

Pip asks Joe if Miss Havisham is 'dead' (459). Joe replies with as much tact as he possesses that 'she ain't living', adding some dark humour to the chapter (459). However, before she died, Joe relates, Miss Havisham 'wrote out a little coddle shell [...] leaving a cool four thousand to Mr. Matthew Pocket' (460). It appears that she had a heart, after all, as a 'coddleshell' is an addition to a will.

The writer appropriately rewards good characters, while punishing the malevolent, like Orlick, as Joe tells Pip: 'Orlick's in the county jail' (461).

Joe takes the sick Pip to convalesce in the countryside of Kent, lifting him out and carrying him 'so easily', as if the latter were St Christopher (462). Given that the saint is the patron of travellers, it appears that the link may not be coincidental.

Joe clearly accepts Pip as a human being, and does not require a full explanation of what happened to him, as he considers it: 'onnecessary' (463). Joe's grammatical errors make him appear a more honest and genuine character than Pip, who has at least mended his ways.

However, the social distance between the two characters cannot be bridged, as Pip admits: 'As I became stronger and better, Joe became a little less easy with me' (464). They are only equal, in terms of status, when Pip is weak. Pip fully appreciates Joe again, admitting he feels 'thankful' that he had been ill. It seems to have given him a chance to reflect on his mistakes (465).

Before Pip leaves, Joe goes to considerable effort to compose a letter to him, which ends: 'P.S. Ever the best of friends' (466). It is a simple, homely message that reminds the reader of how much Joe loves him, especially as he has managed to pay all of Pip's debts.

Pip is very much like a prodigal son, as he plans to ask Biddy, whom he hopes to marry, if she can 'receive' him 'like a forgiven child' (467). Once again, Pip seems to get ahead of himself with his great expectations.

Chapter 58

There is a sea change in the reception that Pip receives at the Blue Boar, now that he is 'going out of property' (467). He now has to endure poorer accommodation 'among the pigeons' (467). It reminds the reader of the canary yellow uniform of his 'Avenger', earlier in the narrative. Pip can no longer preen himself like an expensive bird. He has to opt for rude home truths, like a homing pigeon.

Pumblechook initially appears not to care that Pip's fortunes have suffered a downturn though, as the hand-shaking motif appears again, with the actor extending 'his hand with a magnificently forgiving air' (468). However, Pip seems a bit dismayed by 'the ostentatious clemency with which he had just now exhibited the same fat five fingers' that shook his hand when he was enjoying 'his new prosperity' (469).

Pumblechook reminds Pip of his humble origins and reveals Pip's sister's name 'was Georgiana M'ria', finally ending the mystery of Mrs Joe (470). Pumblechook goes on to mention 'the finger of Providence', which effectively personifies luck by capitalising it and giving it a hand (471). Magwitch's influence on Pip's life was almost like divine intervention, so although Pip objects to Pumblechook mentioning 'Providence', the reference is a fair one. It also links to Magwitch's pseudonym, Provis.

The scene changes to 'the forge', where Pip notes there is no 'clink of Joe's hammer' (472). The lack of sound imagery signifies that something has dramatically changed. It is revealed, much to Pip's consternation, that Joe and Biddy are 'married' (472).

-
- Fate has played its part in bringing Pip to them on their happy day, as he admits he had 'come by accident to make their day complete!' The exclamation mark seems to reveal that Pip's frustration that his passion for Biddy can no longer be expressed. The

question in the reader's mind may be why did they not invite Pip to the wedding?

-

- Nevertheless, Pip asks for forgiveness from both of them, saying: 'Pray tell me, both, that you forgive me!' (474). This seems to be a theme in the novel, as Miss Havisham begs Pip's forgiveness, before she dies.

Pip then reveals that as time passes he lives 'frugally' with 'Herbert and his wife', which would have been a state of affairs much admired by Victorians (474). Although Herbert and Pip are successful, they don't make 'mints of money' (475). The alliterative 'm' softly reminds the reader how it is better not to make too much money and risk losing touch with one's real friends, as Pip did with Joe, earlier in the narrative.

Chapter 59

The narrator's next visit 'eleven years' later to Joe's, allows the reader to discover that Joe has named his son after Pip (475).

Pip moves on to look at the remains of Satis House. The 'old ivy' that has 'struck root anew' seems to offer Pip hope for the future (476). They seem to be the green shoots of his recovery.

Nevertheless, the 'cold silvery mist' makes the scene appear gothic, especially when he beholds 'a solitary figure' (477). It is Estella, who admits she has 'often thought of' Pip (478). She also admits these ruins are her 'only possession' that she has not 'relinquished', seemingly reeling from her disastrous marriage with Drummle.

Although she remains distant, it appears there may be hope of another wedding on the horizon, as Pip takes her 'hand' and sees 'the shadow of no parting from her' (479). However, the reader may wonder if the shadow warns of a future parting from her.

Essay writing tips

Use a variety of connectives

Have a look of this list of connectives. Which of these would you choose to use?

'ADDING' DISCOURSE MARKERS

- AND

- ALSO

- AS WELL AS

- MOREOVER

- TOO

- FURTHERMORE

- ADDITIONALLY

I hope you chose 'additionally', 'furthermore' and 'moreover'. Don't be afraid to use the lesser discourse markers, as they are also useful. Just avoid using those ones over and over again. I've seen essays from Key Stage 4 students that use the same discourse marker for the opening sentence of each paragraph! Needless to say, those essays didn't get great marks!

Okay, here are some more connectives for you to look at. Select the best ones.

'SEQUENCING' DISCOURSE MARKERS

- NEXT

- FIRSTLY

- SECONDLY

- THIRDLY

- FINALLY

- MEANWHILE

- AFTER

- THEN

- SUBSEQUENTLY

This time, I hope you chose 'subsequently' and 'meanwhile'.

Here are some more connectives for you to 'grade'!

'ILLUSTRATING / EXEMPLIFYING' DISCOURSE MARKERS

- FOR EXAMPLE

- SUCH AS

- FOR INSTANCE

- IN THE CASE OF

- AS REVEALED BY

- ILLUSTRATED BY

I'd probably go for 'illustrated by' or even 'as exemplified by' (which is not in the list!). Please feel free to add your own examples to the lists. Strong connectives impress examiners. Don't forget it! That's why I want you to look at some more.

'CAUSE & EFFECT' DISCOURSE MARKERS

- BECAUSE
- SO
- THEREFORE
- THUS
- CONSEQUENTLY
- HENCE

I'm going for 'consequently' this time. How about you? What about the next batch?

'COMPARING' DISCOURSE MARKERS

- SIMILARLY
- LIKEWISE
- AS WITH
- LIKE
- EQUALLY
- IN THE SAME WAY

I'd choose 'similarly' this time. Still some more to go.

'QUALIFYING' DISCOURSE MARKERS

- BUT

- HOWEVER

- WHILE

- ALTHOUGH

- UNLESS

- EXCEPT

- APART FROM

- AS LONG AS

It's 'however' for me!

'CONTRASTING' DISCOURSE MARKERS

- WHEREAS

- INSTEAD OF

- ALTERNATIVELY

- OTHERWISE

- UNLIKE

- ON THE OTHER HAND

- CONVERSELY

I'll take 'conversely' or 'alternatively' this time.

'EMPHASISING' DISCOURSE MARKERS

- ABOVE ALL

- IN PARTICULAR

- ESPECIALLY

- SIGNIFICANTLY

- INDEED

- NOTABLY

You can breathe a sigh of relief now! It's over! No more connectives. However, now I want to put our new found skills to use in our essays.

Specific IGCSE and GCSE essay planning

Let's imagine you have to write an essay in answer to the following question: **To what extent does Dickens portray Pip as a sympathetic character?**

If you look at the whole novel, you can see that in this bildungsroman, Pip has a combination of sympathetic and unsympathetic qualities. However, just looking at the first six chapters, I would come up with the following sub-headings:

Setting:
The dismal setting that Dickens places Pip in makes us immediately feel sorry for the protagonist. Unlike the writer's geographically accurate descriptions of London, Dickens, perhaps deliberately, gives no identifiable places names for the marshes of the Hoo Peninsula. Like Mrs Joe, in the early part of the narrative, they seem even more oppressive due to the fact that they are nameless. This links to the idea of the gothic novel, which often uses the 'unspeakable' to create an idea of horror that defies description. Additionally, by not giving the reader exact locations for the action on the marshes, Dickens is able to use poetic licence to make this Kentish fenland, which is full of muddy ditches, rushes and rank vegetation, seem even more inhospitable than it really is.

Home sweet home?
Mrs Joe is a domestic tyrant and although we may find Dickens ironic use of the name 'Ticker' to describe the stick that she uses to beat Pip with amusing, nevertheless we cannot help but feel

sympathetic towards this violently abused orphan. Dickens used orphans as protagonists in his previous novels, such as: 'Oliver Twist' and 'The Old Curiosity Shop'. The use of a young orphan protagonist proved to be extremely effective, which was evidenced in the national outpouring of grief over Little Nell's death in the latter novel. Through letters received from his readers, Dickens had learned that he had moved them to tears with this kind of characterisation. In later years, Dickens was accused of being overly sentimental in his handling of Little's Nell's death, in particular, with Oscar Wilde famously noting that you would have to have 'a heart of stone not to read the death of Little Nell without dissolving into tears...of laughter'. However, it is more difficult to accuse Dickens of over-sentimentalising Pip's plight, as the injection of grotesque humour of the aforementioned 'Ticker', for example, makes him appear a more well-rounded character, especially as it is combined with an adult first-person narrative which offers a slightly detached view of the child's view of the world.

Pip's name
While being a memorable palindrome, which could serve the writer's purposes of creating unforgettable names in a serialisation such as this, Pip can symbolise a tiny seed starting on life's journey. This,

in itself, can evoke sympathy in the reader, as it is natural to want to take care of something or someone diminutive in stature.

Mrs Joe's treatment of Pip

Like Bishop Berkeley (1685-1753), Mrs Joe adheres to what was, even in Pip's time, the outdated idea that 'Tar-water' was some kind of 'elixir' or panacea, which when 'administered' would cure almost anything. In Mrs Joe's case, she uses it as punishment for Pip 'bolting' his food. Of course, he is not guilty of swallowing without chewing, so the reader feels more sympathy for Pip, who is being harshly and unjustly punished for something he did not do. Although Berkeley believed that children should receive a smaller dosage of Tar-water than adults, Mrs Joe decides to administer a pint of Tar-water to Pip, making him smell 'like a new fence'. This humourous image may remind the reader of Pip's lack of freedom and the idea that he is still fenced in by relative poverty and a lack of a nurturing home life. This generates a sympathetic response in the reader.

Pip's lack of freedom also extends to his clothing. It appears that his sister instructs tailors, when Pip needs a new suit, to 'make them like a kind of Reformatory' so he can 'on no account [...] have the free use of' his 'limbs'. The use of hyperbole makes the narrative amusing, while also emphasising the fact that Pip is metaphorically and literally imprisoned and condemned to live a life of misery by Mrs Joe.

Pip's guilt
When Pip sees the black ox 'with a white cravat on', the protagonist is reminding us of the guilt he feels for the crime he is committing: stealing. Clergymen wore white collars, so the ox represents religious authority that would condemn his actions.

However, it could be argued that Pip is doing something morally wrong for the right reasons, by feeding a fellow human being in need. Then again, if we consider that the person being fed is a potentially dangerous, escaped 'convict', who has already threatened Pip, we may decide that the protagonist is foolishly mistaken, if he thinks he on the moral high ground.

As readers, we may be disappointed at Pip's decision to steal, which may lesson our sympathy for him. Much depends on how sympathetically we view Magwitch, whose body is described as 'shuddering' at the end of chapter one. Of course, it is hard not to sympathise with a fellow human being suffering in this way, particularly as Magwitch appears to have 'got the ague' by chapter three, presumably from exposure to mosquitoes on the marshes. Therefore, a large proportion of readers are bound to think that Pip did the right thing, particularly as Joe, who possibly represents Dickens's view of how people should behave, wishes that Magwitch could evade capture. Joe's Christian forgiveness of a 'poor miserable fellow-creatur' in chapter five exemplifies the moral road that Dickens appears to want the reader to tread. This charitable thought is juxtaposed against those that derive sadistic pleasure from hunting down the convicts, described by the sergeant as 'wild beasts'. This clearly makes the reader sympathetic to Pip's stealing, as it appears to be justified by Joe's opinion.

Given that that 'a party of soldiers' led by an unprofessional 'sergeant', who proceeds to get drunk and make small talk with Pumblechook while on duty, are responsible for apprehending Magwitch and Compeyson, it is hard to have sympathy for the forces of law and order. This lack of belief in the morality of the law enforcement is compounded by the fact that the sergeant declares that he is 'on a chase in the name of the king'. The king at that time was George III, referred to in an 1819 Shelley sonnet as 'old, mad, blind, despised and dying'. Thus, instead of making the reader want to see Magwitch punished and brought to justice 'in the name of the king', Dickens positions us as readers to have more sympathy for the underdog, which in this case is Pip and Magwitch.

By contrast, the law is parodied, even as early as chapter four when the narrator muses that his sister 'must have had some general idea that' Pip 'was a young offender whom an Accoucheur Policeman had taken up [...] and delivered over to her, to be dealt with according to the outraged majesty of the law'. The word 'Accoucher' means male midwife and, by mixing it with the word 'Policeman', Dickens appears to be ridiculing law enforcement at the time.

Animal imagery
Both Pip and Magwitch are compared with dogs throughout the text. Magwitch is described taking 'strong sharp sudden bites just like the dog', mentioned earlier in chapter three. Meanwhile, in chapter one, Magwitch calls Pip: 'You young dog'. These animals are traditionally associated with loyalty, which makes both characters appear sympathetic in the eyes of the reader.

However, it could be argued that Pip's link with the criminal, Magwitch, makes his slightly less sympathetic, but that depends on the individual's view of convicts. Clearly, Dickens wants us to side with Magwitch, at least, as later the narrator refers to him as 'my convict' in chapter five.

Additionally, the narrator's comparison to himself as 'an unfortunate little bull in a Spanish arena' highlights how much he suffering in chapter four. Although he is not being stabbed and prodded physically by the guests at the Christmas dinner, the accumulation of verbal blows are clearly taking their toll on young Pip, making the reader have even more sympathy for his plight.

Pip's violent thoughts
Although Pip's admission that he would like 'pull' Wopsle's 'Roman nose [...] until he howled' is amusing, it does make us question how moral a person Pip is. Nevertheless, the first-person narrative is more likely to make us side with Pip than not, so we can accept his aggressive thoughts, particularly given that he has been treated so poorly by Mrs Joe and nearly all the assembled company in chapter four. What makes Pip's treatment worse (for example, him being compared to 'Swine') is the fact that it is supposed to a Christmas dinner, a festive occasion associated with kindness, rather than name-calling.

Of course, I would advise you to re-arrange these sub-titles in an order that suits the points you are trying to make about Pip. Please remember, also, that the sub-titles above only refer to the opening six chapters.

Additional note on the serialisation
The serialisation began in the publication called 'All the Year Round' with the first chapters of 'Great Expectations' being published on 1st December 1860. Usually, the weekly installments would contain two chapters, except for when Dickens wrote a longer chapter (as is the case with chapters: 8, 11, 18, 19, 22, 29, 38, 39, 40, 53, 54, and 57).

Useful information/Glossary

Allegory: extended metaphor, like the grim reaper representing death, e.g. Scrooge symbolizing capitalism.

Alliteration: same consonant sound repeating, e.g. 'She sells sea shells'.

Allusion: reference to another text/person/place/event.

Ascending tricolon: sentence with three parts, each increasing in power, e.g. 'ringing, drumming, shouting'.

Aside: character speaking so some characters cannot hear what is being said. Sometimes, an aside is directly to the audience. It's a dramatic technique which reveals the character's inner thoughts and feelings.

Assonance: same vowel sounds repeating, e.g. 'Oh no, won't Joe go?'

Bathos: abrupt change from sublime to ridiculous for humorous effect.

Blank verse: lines of unrhymed iambic pentameter.

Compressed time: when the narrative is fast-forwarding through the action.

Descending tricolon: sentence with three parts, each decreasing in power, e.g. 'shouting, talking, whispering'.

Denouement: tying up loose ends, the resolution.

Diction: choice of words or vocabulary.

Didactic: used to describe literature designed to inform, instruct or pass on a moral message.

Dilated time: opposite compressed time, here the narrative is in slow motion.

Direct address: second person narrative, predominantly using the personal pronoun 'you'.

Dramatic action verb: manifests itself in physical action, e.g. I punched him in the face.

Dramatic irony: audience knows something that the character is unaware of.

Ellipsis: leaving out part of the story and allowing the reader to fill in the narrative gap.

End-stopped lines: poetic lines that end with punctuation.

Epistolary: letter or correspondence-driven narrative.

Flashback/Analepsis: going back in time to the past, interrupting the chronological sequence.

Flashforward/Prolepsis: going forward in time to the future, interrupting the chronological sequence.

Foreshadowing/Adumbrating: suggestion of plot developments that will occur later in the narrative.

Gothic: another strand of Romanticism, typically with a wild setting, a sensitive heroine, an older man with a 'piercing gaze', discontinuous structure, doppelgangers, guilt and the 'unspeakable' (according to Eve Kosofsky Sedgwick).

Hamartia: character flaw, leading to that character's downfall.

Hyperbole: exaggeration for effect.

Iambic pentameter: a line of ten syllables beginning with a lighter stress alternating with a heavier stress in its perfect form, which sounds like a heartbeat. The stress falls on the even syllables, numbers: 2, 4, 6, 8 and 10, e.g. 'When now I think you can behold such sights'.

Intertextuality: links to other literary texts.

Irony: amusing or cruel reversal of expected outcome or words meaning the opposite to their literal meaning.

Metafiction/Romantic irony: self-conscious exposure of the devices used to create 'the truth' within a work of fiction.

Motif: recurring image use of language or idea that connects the narrative together and creates a theme or mood, e.g. 'green light' in *The Great Gatsby*.

Objective correlative: external features of the scene mirroring the feelings of a character.

Oxymoron: contradictory terms combined, e.g. deafening silence.

Pastiche: imitation of another's work.

Pathetic fallacy: a form of personification whereby inanimate objects show human attributes, e.g. 'the sea smiled benignly'. The originator of the term, John Ruskin in 1856, used 'the cruel, crawling foam', from Kingsley's *The Sands of Dee*, as an example to clarify what he meant by the 'morbid' nature of pathetic fallacy.

Personification: concrete or abstract object made human, often simply achieved by using a capital letter or a personal pronoun, e.g. 'Nature', or describing a ship as 'she'.

Pun/Double entendre: a word with a double meaning, usually employed in witty wordplay but not always.

Retrospective: account of events after they have occurred.

Romanticism: genre celebrating the power of imagination, spriritualism and nature.

Semantic/lexical field: related words about a single concept, e.g. king, queen and prince are all concerned with royalty.

Soliloquy: character thinks aloud, but is not heard by other characters (unlike in a monologue) giving the audience access to inner thoughts and feelings.

Style: choice of language, form and structure, and effects produced.

Synecdoche: one part of something referring to the whole, e.g. Carker's teeth represent him in *Dombey and Son*.

Syntax: the way words and sentences are placed together.

Tetracolon climax: sentence with four parts, culminating with the last part, e.g. 'I have nothing to offer but blood, toil, tears, and sweat ' (Winston Churchill).

ABOUT THE AUTHOR

Joe Broadfoot is a secondary school teacher of English and a soccer journalist, who also writes fiction and literary criticism. His former experiences as a DJ took him to far-flung places such as Tokyo, Kobe, Beijing, Hong Kong, Jakarta, Cairo, Dubai, Cannes, Oslo, Bergen and Bodo. He is now PGCE and CELTA-qualified with QTS, a first-class honours degree in Literature and an MA in Victorian Studies (majoring in Charles Dickens). Drama is close to his heart as he acted in 'Macbeth' and 'A Midsummer Night's Dream' at the Royal Northern College of Music in Manchester. More recently, he has been teaching 'A' Level and GCSE English Literature and IGCSE and GCSE English Language to students at secondary schools in Buckinghamshire, Kent and in south and west London.

Printed in Great Britain
by Amazon

21975411R10096